The
UNDELIVERED
MARDLE

A MEMOIR OF BELIEF, DOUBT
AND DELIGHT

JOHN ROGERS

DARTON · LONGMAN + TODD

John Rogers lives in Suffolk and is a
retired teacher and tree planter. He is also
author of *The Basic Bible* (Hutchinson).

First published in 2012 by
Darton, Longman and Todd Ltd
1 Spencer Court
140 – 142 Wandsworth High Street
London SW18 4JJ

ISBN 978-0-232-52956-2

A catalogue record for this book is available from the British Library.

Designed and typeset by Judy Linard
Printed and bound by Scandbook AB

I dedicate this book to those most cordial people of Letheringham who have let me write about the things they say and do, and to many other magnanimous friends and acquaintances who have patiently helped me in the making of it.

CONTENTS

INTRODUCTION

This wry soliloquy on rural Christianity takes place in a corner of Suffolk which was my home for many years, and of which I still myself feel a part. It is a remarkable confession, beautifully written and quite unlike the myriad accounts I have read of a village church. Truth vies with uncertainty, experience with imagination. A heart attack set it going, releasing a confusion of belief, doubt – and delight. What we all most dread, the pain from nowhere on an ordinary pleasant day, comes bearing gifts of the spirit. Everyone who worships in an ancient parish church, or haunts it, Pevsner in hand, or with Philip Larkin in his head, should read it, for it says many things which have not been said, at least so openly. Intimations of mortality, via Papworth, can do wonders for the soul, particularly if one writes well.

They made John Rogers take stock of what might be described as his priestly side – to tell his story of mardle. Although I am not sure if it is accurate, Suffolk has a reputation for silence – unless some tale sets the words flowing. Certainly there are people renowned as storytellers, other than those famed as gossips, that is. The heart attack intervened when it came to John Rogers' turn to tell a mardle in the village hall so in time it grew into this memoir, heaven obviously having a hand in it. It is not a story any of us will forget. Churchgoing will not be the same after one has read it, whether for worship or for architecture. Or in John Rogers' case for encounters. He is the kind of man who meets an angel unawares, usually on his bike, or scything grass, or after the eight o'clock Holy Communion. The joy of *The Undelivered Mardle* is that though intimate, it is expansive. We may accompany the author through the farmyard to the church at Letheringham Abbey but we will travel to Jerusalem on the way.

Few of our East Anglian churches can have been given such a battering as Letheringham. But it hung on, its sacredness intact. There it was on the hillside every time I passed, murmuring something Augustinian, something maybe in Chaucer's tongue, something I understood. Being lay-chairman of the Loes Deanery Synod, it was especially precious to me but I was waiting for its explanation, and here it is. I could have supplied all the Norman and Perp, but it took a brush with extinction to supply the rest. His adventure makes John Rogers rehearse the tenets of his Anglicanism. 'I believe in …' What does he believe in? What do you or I believe in as we face east? And how have these beliefs come to Letheringham – and remained there? The lady who does the flowers doesn't know. But the stranger within its gate is apt to make an accurate stab at the right answer. Of course it means a witty trail through liturgy, the hymnal, and some light though not lightly understood theology.

All this with a kind of serious playfulness which makes *The Undelivered Mardle* a serious read. The Jesus who emerges from all this is young and fresh, as he was when we were children, and before we grew out of him.

There has been no end to the ways in which faith has been found and re-found. Or searched for in a neglected shrine. Whilst London churches were burning in World War II, T S Eliot told us to kneel 'where prayer has been valid' in a remote church at Little Gidding. Such buildings litter the map of these islands and all of them have something imperishable to say to us. In the changed universe which follows an illness the eloquence of a little Suffolk farmyard church was heard, and this is what it said.

Ronald Blythe

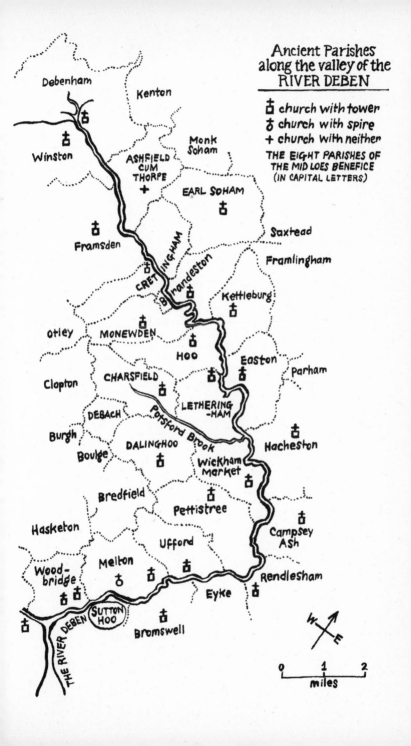

Ancient Parishes
along the valley of the
RIVER DEBEN

✠ church with tower
♱ church with spire
✝ church with neither

THE EIGHT PARISHES OF
THE MID LOES BENEFICE
(IN CAPITAL LETTERS)

Debenham

Kenton

Winston

Monk
Soham

ASHFIELD
CUM
THORPE

EARL SOHAM

Framsden

Saxtead

CRETINGHAM

Brandeston

Framlingham

Kettleburg

Otley

MONEWDEN

HOO

Easton

Parham

Clopton

CHARSFIELD

LETHERING
-HAM

DEBACH

Potsford Brook

Burgh

DALINGHOO

Boulge

Wickham
Market

Hacheston

Bredfield

Pettistree

Hasketon

Ufford

Campsey
Ash

Woodbridge

Melton

Rendlesham

SUTTON
HOO

Eyke

Bromswell

THE RIVER DEBEN

W E

0   1   2
miles

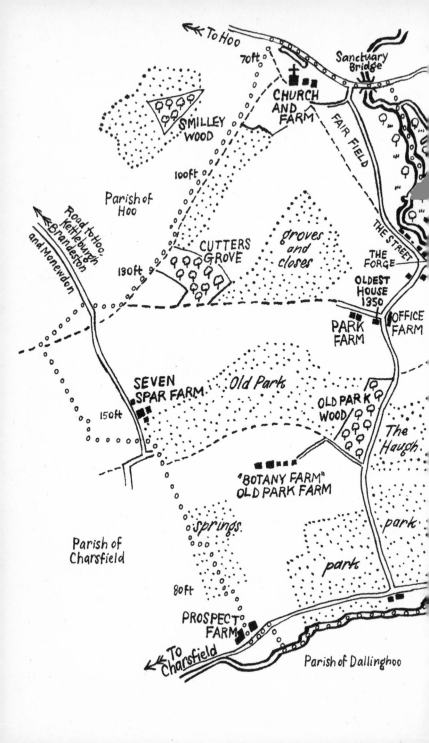

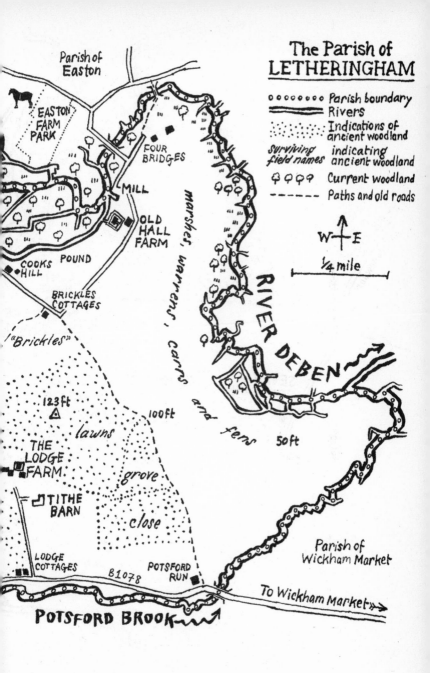

The Parish of
LETHERINGHAM

o o o o o o o o o   Parish boundary
⎯⎯⎯⎯⎯   Rivers
:::::::::   Indications of ancient woodland
surviving field names   indicating ancient woodland
♀ ♀ ♀ ♀   Current woodland
⎯ ⎯ ⎯ ⎯   Paths and old roads

W ↑ E

¼ mile

Parish of Easton

Easton Farm Park

Four Bridges

Mill

Old Hall Farm

Pound

Cooks Hill

Brickles Cottages

"Brickles"

marshes, warrens, carrs and fens

RIVER DEBEN

123 ft

lawns

100 ft

50 ft

The Lodge Farm

grove

Tithe Barn

close

Lodge Cottages

B1078

Potsford Run

Parish of Wickham Market

To Wickham Market »

POTSFORD BROOK

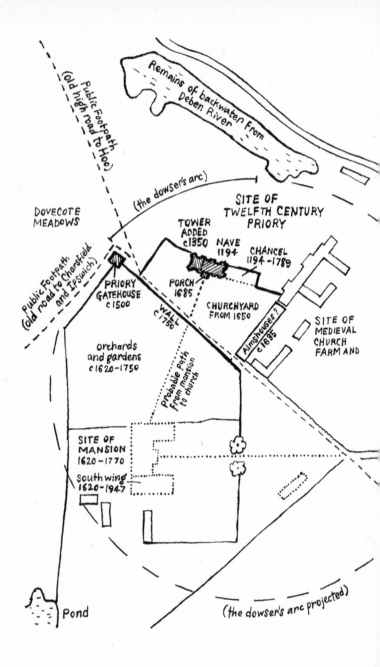

Public Footpath (old high road to Hoo)

Remains of backwater from Deben River

(the dowser's arc)

SITE OF TWELFTH CENTURY PRIORY

DOVECOTE MEADOWS

TOWER ADDED c1350

NAVE 1194

CHANCEL 1194-1789

Public Footpath (old road to Charsfield and Ipswich)

PRIORY GATEHOUSE c1500

PORCH 1685

WALL c1750

CHURCHYARD FROM 1650

orchards and gardens c1620-1750

Probable path from mansion to church

Almshouses? c1685

SITE OF MEDIEVAL CHURCH FARM AND

SITE OF MANSION 1620-1770

south wing 1620-1947

Pond

(the dowser's arc projected)

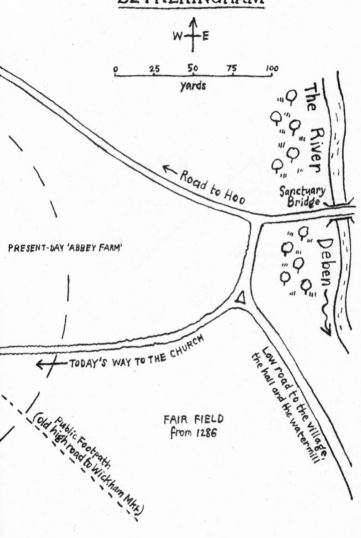

The Priory Church of St Mary LETHERINGHAM

W — E

0   25   50   75   100
yards

The River

Road to Hoo

Sanctuary Bridge

Deben

PRESENT-DAY 'ABBEY FARM'

TODAY'S WAY TO THE CHURCH

Low road to the village, the hall and the watermill

FAIR FIELD from 1286

Public Footpath (old high road to Wickham Mkt)

Chapter 1
MARDLING

At about dawn on the Monday I called an ambulance. It came quickly and we clattered away to Ipswich. They dosed me with morphine, instant relief from the pain. In the hospital they muttered among themselves, shook their heads and packed me off to Papworth near Cambridge in another ambulance, a bigger vehicle, faster and noisier, with flashing blue lights, scaring lorries and motorbikes into ditches. There was a man in green with me and a nurse who fixed sensors to my chest and, I learned later, the information gained was being transmitted by radio to the surgeons in Papworth as they sharpened their knives. The nurse was crying, I don't know why. I thought she looked pretty crying.

They gave me more morphine and, becoming very sleepy, I blissfully surrendered my soul to the Almighty, yet still half conscious, going in and out of sleep, no longer feeling the pain and not the slightest bit frightened. In fact it was a most exciting sensation, being about to undergo my own death, and I was eager to be taken over by the great dream. There were none of the ghastly pangs we suffer at the deathbed of friends and relations, only a vague regret that I had left things untidily behind for others to clear up.

I did not die: they inserted a couple of stents near the heart via the groin and I was given ten days of five-star hospital treatment entirely free, which humbled me. I must live a better life, I thought, worthy of such undeserved bounty, such grace.

The heart attack had come on Monday 26th March 2007, the Feast of St William of Norwich, and that very evening at Easton Farm Park across the river I was expected to give a talk for the people of Letheringham, which had taken many weeks to prepare. They quickly found a good substitute, a man called Jason from Great Glemham who, I am told, talked eloquently about Borneo.

These talks are monthly and they are called mardles, the Suffolk word for gossips. People pay £6 and the money goes to the upkeep of the Priory Church at Letheringham. I do not know why they asked me to deliver a mardle. The expression reminded me of Piers Plowman coughing up a caudle. A resourceful parishioner called Polly ffitch said she thought I was a parson and would perform well, but I have never been a parson. I have been a tree planter and a schoolmaster but, as a public speaker, I am unpredictable and it terrifies me. I think the reason why I accepted the invitation must have been that I am vain and was flattered to be asked. Besides, the subject interested me. It was to have been about the little Priory Church at Letheringham and I wanted to question the sense of preserving such relics, and they said I could. I also said I wanted to talk about trees, scandals, and the future, and they allowed that too. But since the heart attack I have felt rather feeble and have decided I can more easily write it down than deliver it at some later date. So this is it.

The church was built about 800 years ago as part of a small priory, a satellite of the great Augustinian abbey in Ipswich, ten miles to the south-west. An official notice at the entrance to the churchyard proclaims that there were only three monks who were canons, not priests, and they were either 'old, ill or naughty'. I wonder where this information came from. It seems dubious to me. I suppose naughty could mean they were penniless. For the first 350 years the priory prospered until the Reformation when it was dissolved and burnt. Thereafter the remaining church was pillaged, abused and neglected until it became a ruin and, after repairs in about 1800, amazingly it stands today intact, though reduced, and in healthy basic running order. That is its history.

Chapter 2
THE APPROACH

I had been to see the church for the first time three months earlier, just after Christmas 2006 and it looked to me that day, in its isolation, like a small stray creature crouching on a windswept brow, mute and abandoned, a winter version of Tessa Newcomb's delightful painting. The door was unlocked, and there was no one inside. It was warm after the wind outside and flooded with soft horizontal light from the lowering sun. Clear glass windows, whitewashed walls, boxed pinewood pews, a patched-up wooden pulpit on the left, a small altar table in the east with unusual rails, a handful of memorials.

I stopped looking and sat down. I asked no questions but simply waited, breathing deeply, pleased to rest. I thought, I would like to go back 800 years and be among those people who were building the priory, to hear their voices and watch what they were doing, see exactly how they handled their chisels, their hammers, their levers and pulleys. The labourers were largely local Anglo-Saxons, I presumed, some with a little Danish blood perhaps, outnumbering the monks from Ipswich. I might catch sight of the Norman landowner, their patron, William de Bovile when he came up from the Old Hall to inspect the progress.

I imagined approaching the site from the south-east with the morning sun behind me. The sundial was not yet in place, and no clocks to tell the time, no tower, no bells – except probably a hand-held Angelus at midday; no aircraft or traffic, no familiar sounds or scents. Instead perhaps the earthy pounding of oxen working nearby, the light percussion of their harness, a shouting boy, and people in the yard to the right tending pigs and goats. Would it be winter? Could I choose, it would be May and I would notice, as I passed, the great diversity of flowers and their greenery, hear the bees and their comrades framed in the deep blue silence of a motorless world, hear clearly the cries of the crows, the distant curlew. And, nearing the builders, I'd hear the beat of iron on oak and stone, of stone on flint, and the lapping of water on the boats below, smell the wet clay and the smoke of hornbeam in a kiln of soft red bricks.

When they saw me coming what would they say? They would stop work at once. They would confer among themselves, and would they take fright? I would have to tread cautiously, no sudden movements, go as to a herd of kine. And they would assess me as an animal does, not noticing my strange clothes or my greater height or my outward appearance so much as sensing instinctively my true self and intentions. I once worked with an old forester from Cumberland, Bob Ray, who could do just that. Words were of secondary importance to him because he knew what was going on, what people were thinking, who was good and who was not so good.

The purpose of my visit had been from the start to discover their thoughts and intentions: why were they building this thing? I could see the reason in a house or a barn or a boat, but why did such lowly people spend their precious energies on this? And why in this place? I wanted to ask what they believed about life and their place in the world, and perhaps even to ask their opinion about our way of life today, our comparative godlessness. But as I stood there before them, I realised that such cerebral exercises were barbaric to them. The Lollards were not to come for at least another hundred years and such words as atheist even later. Our modern outlook simply could not be contained within their mental framework. So I felt rather silly standing there and it seemed only polite to roll up my sleeves and help. This I did and soon was taken over with such feelings of warmth and wellbeing as I have seldom known before. They taught me so eagerly, and so sympathetic were they with my shortcomings, that after a very short time I thought I had spent my whole life with them. I learnt that you can do whatever you wish with a piece of clay or wood or stone so long as you respect its nature, obey its rules; you have in your mind's eye an intention, your hands and your tools are willing labourers, but the judge and measure of your work is the material itself, and its own compliance with the natural laws of the planet. So you work in partnership, and you are the junior partner.

These thoughts dawned on me as I worked and supped and slept with them. From the earliest times the Christians had taught them the mantras I heard them chanting: '…O Father in heaven …. give us this day our daily bread … thou openest thy hand and fillest all things living with plenteousness … Working is praying and prayer is work … Thy will be done, on earth as in heaven … By their fruits ye shall know them …'. For me to question their hierarchy of heaven and earth would have been anathema and they would probably have regarded me as a lunatic and cast me out like the vagabond that I was. Simply to mention the modern ideas of godlessness would have been rough and rude, an insult to their hospitality, and this I was determined to avoid, such was my enjoyment of their society.

The following week I was sent out with Joseph and his brethren to find flints in the fields above the river and one afternoon, while engaged in that hard task, I decided to stop thinking about our modern predicaments and concentrate on the matter in hand. In today's world people tend to regard any work that a machine cannot do, any plain manual labour, as demeaning. But no such thought crossed the minds of the flint pickers. They just longed to get back to the site with it, knapping it, unlocking its treasures without damaging it, displaying its strengths and glories in their walls. To them, talking about it in these terms would seem peculiar; they simply got on and did it. I found that such skills demand undivided concentration. No room for daydreams or sophistry. You give your all and are transported in a process which pays you with a wordless wisdom, the sort that my dear

Cumberland forester had. It is not a cerebral commodity but physical, and needs no words. I have seen brilliant tractor drivers working with it today.

Then I stopped thinking that afternoon in Letheringham. My thoughts about the builders were all too busy for such a place and I put them firmly aside and waited till more time passed. A bird in the eaves somewhere behind was fluttering but I did not turn. Then with no warning at all I find I am in a daydream, a trance, borne aloft to and fro, my breathing like the movement of waters, weightless and sublime. And in my floating body I seem to know the true measure of things and my brain has no part in this knowledge. The pale evening nave of that small place holds me like my mother's arms and I am newborn, safe and wholly nourished.

The trance may have lasted a split second or fifteen minutes, I do not know, but I came to realise that the nature of it was precisely the same as the sensation I was to have thirteen weeks later in the rackety ambulance travelling westwards. And the questions that have to be asked about such a place are to be found in that threshold of timelessness. Everybody has been there one way or another. There is nothing difficult or unusual about it.

Outside the church I looked back. Only half of what remained had been built by those 'naughty monks' eight hundred years before, for the porch and the tower had been added later, and the nave that I was looking at was the lesser part of what they originally built because to its right had stood a larger chancel. The chancel had been the more important part because that was where the monks used to worship morning, noon and night. It was separated from the nave by a screen. The local villagers and the pilgrims from Ipswich and elsewhere were allowed to observe them through the screen. The contractor, who saved the nave from ruin six hundred years later, dismantled their chancel and probably rebuilt its east window where it is now, sealing off the poor little decapitated nave with which we are left today. So today we have to imagine through the clear glass of that east window the chanting of the Latin Mass and the lesser offices; but it is less easy for us to imagine what they thought they gained thereby, what they thought they were up to, for we today are very different creatures indeed.

Roger Keene, a retired architect, lives in the village of Letheringham and is one of the church's leading lights. He says that the limestone that they used could have been shipped up the river, the Deben, via Woodbridge and Wickham Market, imported from either Caen in Normandy or Lincolnshire. I feel sure the Deben must have been wider in those days – the Alde where I live in Rendham certainly was. Maybe it was beginning to divide and if, as I guess, one of its branches went by the Priory, that would explain the now-isolated site; their fish traps would have amply supplied a major ingredient in their diet. The site is also half a mile upstream from the nearest houses, and down in the village there is thought to have been a Saxon church near the old mill, probably built of wood. These things suggest private interests in the building of our priory. Monasticism was after all a commercial enterprise, though not in the modern sense. Christianity had loosely made its way across Europe since the very beginning but monasteries were the first practical application of it in serious business terms. It paid its way but it was benevolent in intent, taking in outsiders, feeding and clothing them, healing and educating and inspiring them to live their lives in harmony with the laws of heaven. Each monastery built up a local 'welfare state', a practical and sophisticated form of Christianity which had come to East Anglia in about AD600 and established communities of both men and women. These however had been reduced greatly by the Vikings. The Norman Conquest had been followed by new waves of Cistercians and Augustinians in particular, so Letheringham Priory was a small ripple from one of those waves, although it is probable that the newcomers built upon a pre-Viking site.

Monasticism was a reaction to the popularisation of Christianity by the Roman Emperor Constantine in AD325. The original idea behind monasticism came from an Egyptian hermit, St Antony (about 250-350), who aimed through extreme austerity to dwell on the simple teachings of Jesus of Nazareth. It was adapted by St Benedict, (about 500-550) to become the basis of all monastic orders in the Western Church. He made rules about poverty, purity and piety but the practical axis of monastic life was the complementary principle of work and worship. The interaction of work and worship was thought, like the Yin and Yang of Chinese philosophy, to maintain the harmony of the community and of the individual. To work was to pray, they said, and praying was their work. This made such practical sense to them that they had no need to question it.

About a hundred years before this priory church was built, Domesday recorded a population of 130 and it remained about that for centuries until the Industrial Revolution when it began to decline towards its present size of 65, strung out, as it always has been, along the river's south bank from the settlement at the Priory in the northwest to the Mill and the Old Hall three quarters of a mile to the east; and later, isolated farmsteads were added away to the south – Park Farm and Office Farm – and over the hill and down to the Brook from the Potsford fens – the Lodge and its Tithe Barn across to Prospect Farm in the southwest – all of which one by one appeared, as clearings were made in the woodland.

At the time of the Conquest only about two hundred acres were farmed and all the rest was woodland, with warrens and wetlands along the river. According to Domesday the diet was varied: game, pork, lamb, a little beef, a lot of rabbit, fish in plenty, goats' milk and flesh but not much cows' milk; honey, pigeons and, later, farmed pigeon eggs and poultry; nuts and berries from the woods, cultivated fruit, abundant wild plants and herbs alongside their own crops of grain and roots, and a brave range of things brewed and fermented. The most cultivated crop by far was oats, being the fuel for their working oxen and horses, then barley and, least of all, wheat. That order remained much the same until the nineteenth century when it was reversed by the discovery of steam power and oil, and by the alarming demands of expanding human populations in the towns. Until the Industrial Revolution all fodder had its seasons and every glut was matched with a dearth. So stable communities ate and stored their food with circumspection, and few died of obesity. Their way of life for centuries had been to live in this harmony with the rhythm of the seasons – at times they might have said, in fear of and in obedience to it – and it had been so since Pagan times and long before any history was written down. That rhythm of the seasons remains the sustaining pulse of what goes on to this day inside churches like Letheringham, laid out in their ancient Church Calendar and echoed with relish in their antique songs and devotions. 'The eyes of all wait upon thee, O Lord, and thou givest them their meat in due season', they chant, unperturbed by the relentless work they put into getting it; 'Thou openest thine hand, and fillest all things living with plenteousness', they continue, with words which are at least three thousand years old.

Chapter 3
SYMBOLS

On Monday 22nd January I motored to Easton to attend my first mardle and see how it was done. It was a dark night but there was no mistaking the hall in parkland which for some years had been ingeniously converted to an open farmstead for the entertainment of children of all ages from the pram to the pension. As a visitor the previous summer I had found it entirely charming. So this dark evening we moved between all sorts of sleeping creatures to get to the fun, at the far south end of the yard, in the old dairy.

Penny Butterworth had spent much of her life teaching people embroidery and the hall was decorated with some of her own work. I was captivated by her talk. For me, her most memorable anecdote went roughly as follows: 'I was asked to design and make an altar frontal for a local church ... had never done anything like this before... went round the parish collecting all sorts of materials from the woods and ditches: stones, leaves, reeds, flowers, shells, debris washed aside by the river, sacking, and so on until I felt I had a natural representation of that place ... they had said I could do anything I liked as long as I included five small crosses of a particular design connected with that church's history... Well, you know how church people love symbolism? So I put them together in a sort of abstract way but it contained some strong representations of the important shapes I had seen … When it came to handing the frontal over to The Parochial Church Council they inspected it in great excitement … I heard 'I think it's the crossing of the Red Sea' and 'Isn't that the feeding of the five thousand?' and 'No, no, that's definitely Mount Sinai' and so on… anyway they accepted it enthusiastically and as we left the room and turned out the lights the moon shone brightly through the windows on to the frontal and lit up for the first time the largely concealed crosses which I had depicted in silver … that did the trick – it was a truly magical moment!'

This is how people differ in their perception of the same object. And everyone who visits the church at Letheringham sees it differently according to his or her needs. The scientific part of the mind does not like such inexactitude. It seeks dimensions and time spans that can be measured and recorded accurately. This is why I have felt I must put aside that scientific part of my mind and try to identify motives for building and motifs in what was built and, alongside them, the emotions of those who have used the building down the ages, all their loves and fears, sadnesses and hopes that have gone to give it its character. Its character is an unmeasurable quality which we sense not in our brains but in our bones, a phenomenon which is not readily accessible to scientific enquiry.

But the intentions of the original builders were largely obliterated by the Reformation and the desecration which followed. Their ancient desire had been to give meaning to their processions led by the priest through the west door and up to the high altar, but now the west door was bricked up, the fine stone font was said to have been 'lost'; the rood screen with its carved crucifix torn down, the lectern and pulpit huddled together on one side; the original chancel and choir with the steps up to the sanctuary and the stone altar high in the east all demolished. Only the most important symbolism remains unchangeable. It is the building's orientation to the rising sun, symbol of new life, resurrection and indefatigable optimism.

So the church at Letheringham today retains precious little of its original symbolism. Its only unmistakable Christian sign is the large brass Latin cross on the little wooden altar in the east. The altar itself is a less noticeable sign of Reformation ardour. Made of wood, it is a plain table where a meal takes place in memory of the Last Supper. It probably replaced a stone structure by which the Church of Rome had long since been more eager to emphasise the aspect of sacrifice.

The plain window above the altar contains none of the heavy stained glass that might have marred its new simplicity in 1800, thanks to their lack of restoration funds at the time no doubt. Indeed, the chief architectural characteristic inside the building today is its lofty simplicity with a faintly Georgian flavour. And its decoration is scarce too but for the altar frontals stitched together locally and changed with the seasons, and for the constant vases of flowers – splashes of colour, tokens of the bounteous Lord Above and the gratitude of someone in Letheringham below.

Chapter 4
THE DEAD

My second visit to the church was on Sunday 2nd February at eight o'clock in the morning, because I thought there was to be a service. But I was mistaken, so I wandered around for a couple of hours possibly waiting for something to happen. It did not, but this is what I saw.

The church stands in what some call God's Acre, actually only about two thirds of an acre. It is anciently walled and contains eight or nine trees bullied by the winds, planted about thirty years ago – four rowans, three cherries, a type of horse chestnut, a battered Scots pine and sundry self-seeded elders. Someone more recently has planted a turkey oak in the west. I heard that the grass was cut by a man called Peter who came and went as he chose and would take no payment. I wanted to meet him. But there have also been times not so long ago when sheep cropped the grass – they were, after all, civilization's first lawn mowers.

The oldest grave I could find that day was of a man named Syrad who died in 1711. It seems a long time ago to me. In the next hundred and fifty years there was a Blyth, a Warren, a Borlden and a Borbett; a Cudberd and several Cuthberts, Cracknells and Catchpoles; several Redgraves, Pecks and Smiths, and one Dove. Who were they? Who buried them there and with what intent? In the County Records Office I chanced to meet a man from Bedford called Robert Peck who said he was trying to find where his great-grandfather, Arthur Peck, had lived in Letheringham. He thinks he was a tenant in Forge cottages and was kicked out in 1922 when the Hamiltons sold up, but he lost trace of him till he was buried here in 1929. He knows his family has laboured in this parish for the best part of two hundred years because in 1826 a John Peck married an Eliza Rodgers (there's a coincidence!) and they produced a dozen children.

Right by the church there were more recent graves: Mary Kerr who died in 1975, wife of William Kerr who died 1989. They had come from Ayrshire, the inscription said, in 1938. They must surely be the parents of John Kerr, a farmer I had seen at Penny's mardle. Further east are the graves of the Clarkes, also farmers but Suffolk people who moved into the parish in 1922: Kenneth died in 1974 aged only sixty. Since that, a Bedwell, a Wood and two Youngs among others have died. I wondered who they were and who will come hunting for their graves in a hundred years' time, and why? Why does it matter to us so?

The most noticeable grave was one covered with fresh flowers for a girl named Rebecca Emily Summerhayes Rice who had died on 4th August 2006, 'shockingly' I later heard. She was only eighteen. Entries in the visitors' book refer to her and reveal feelings common to many these days: their most frequent word is Love; next comes Peace, Peaceful Sleep and Sleeping Happily; then Always-remembered and Never-forgotten; and then We pray for you, We miss you and Please pray for us. And then there are the hopes that God will bless Rebecca, that she will be safely in the Hands of God, and With our Lord, and in Heaven; and another says 'Our memories keep you forever, you are just a thought away', and another, 'You are now an angel, Rebs, to give us guidance.'

I went outside again and stood for a long time beside that grave. I saw the bright optimism of the fresh flowers and felt the awful depth of her loss. And I felt the wind about me which had carried messages from that other world since before history was recorded. The church behind me, with the quiet confidence of a broody hen, continued to prepare us all for a safe hatching in that other world. Surely, for this reason alone, she should be kept in good health for the task.

Back in the porch to get warm, I thought of others who do not see things this way, who are uncomfortable with ideas of a world other than the physical and mental; some of them, good friends, are not only uncomfortable but infuriated. They explain emotions in terms of the bio-chemistry of the brain, nothing more. Mercifully, ardent atheists are as rare as obsessive saints. I think the rest of us are the majority bumbling along in the middle, agnostics, waverers, seekers and searchers, and quite a lot of amiable-but-couldn't-care-lessers.

I sympathise with those who cannot bear funeral services – too much verbiage, they say, too complicating when they feel the need for some silence. They say they want to be alone with their grief, and I agree with that too but I think we need also to cope with it collectively sometimes, not all the time. The crux of the Church of England funeral service for me is the quoted words of Job in his grief 2400 years ago, 'The Lord hath given, the Lord hath taken away, blessed be the name of the Lord.' When I hear that I can bear the rest. I mean, if for you there is no Lord in heaven, it still makes complete sense because our lives really can be described as gifts from beyond our ken and to call the giver and taker of life Fate or Chance does no harm to the truth of the drama. The only debatable detail is your view of Chance: is it a curse or a blessing? That is the question.

Inside the porch there is a photograph of Letheringham's Home Guard during the Second World War. There they are, looking out at us across the years, several of them no doubt still known to a few local people, some still alive perhaps. Their names ring out like the heroic roll calls that can be heard in every parish in England: Allum, Beck, Buckles, Cattermole, Clark (not Kenneth Clarke from the Hall, who was absent on that occasion), Clough, Johnson, Kerr (William Kerr that is), Matthew, Martin, Paul, Revell, Smith and Williams. Some of them resemble characters described in Ronald Blythe's book, *Akenfield*, and they are also remarkably similar in appearance to the characters I remember so well in my own childhood in Kent – I was nine at the end of the War. What did they all believe? How did they each cope with the fighting they were preparing for? And, looking back, how did they view their lives? And, as for the church here, how many of them used it for one reason or another – weddings and christenings, Christmases and Easters, harvests, funerals and great emergencies like declarations of war? Which ones had a partiality for Matins or Evensong or Communion, heard the one remaining bell in the tower and responded on occasions to its soft four-hundred-year-old voice each week?

How many, I would really like to know, were persuaded by the growing cynicism of the fifties and sixties to abandon it all? I went into the church to get warmer and there I saw, in the same light as those men in the porch, the two Wingfield brasses of five or six hundred years ago, Sir John looking straight at the camera, a good-natured and patient man I thought, and Sir Thomas with helmet off and flowing locks, bemused and eyeing someone over my right shoulder, both admirably slim in their armour but Tom not so well turned out, rather whimsical with his sword slung amidships, perhaps to disguise his knock knees or some other private proclivity. The official guidebook in the church (one of the best I've ever read) contains excellent depictions of these two gentlemen.

The Wingfields followed by the Nauntons were the landowners who presided over the events in Letheringham for four hundred years from about 1350. The Visitors' Book contains numerous entries from New Zealand, Australia, Canada and the United States of modern travellers who had come specifically to find traces of their Wingfield or Naunton ancestors. An Australian

Wingfield claims to have a list of 2000 descendants and an American one speaks of a 'Wingfield Family Society'. As the Reformation set in, the land passed over from the Wingfields to the Nauntons by marriage and they moved the dominant house up from the Hall to their swanky new mansion by the church in 1620 – the fourth largest in Suffolk – built with materials no doubt from the Priory which had recently been destroyed by fire. They called it Letheringham 'Abbey', though there are no records of such an exalted foundation anywhere near the parish. It was finally demolished in 1947.

These two families lived through the Black Death, the Great Storm at Dunwich, the Dissolution of the Monasteries, the earthquaking translation of the Bible into English, the introduction of the Book of Common Prayer – which involved many executions including that of the archbishop who had compiled it – the Norwich Plague which snatched away one in three persons, the Civil War and the Commonwealth, the Fire of London, the immigration of the Huguenots and the Gin Acts.

In Letheringham they presided over the building of the church tower and the priory gatehouse, the hanging of three church bells, the burning of the priory and the iconoclastic removal of 'Popish items' from the crumbling church, and the building of a south porch to the church, which church however by 1750 was to become 'roofless and expected to fall'. So one has to wonder whether their descendants consider them to have been a good thing or a bad thing.

There is a most moving memorial to the right of the altar. The inscription indicates that little James Naunton 'here sleeps with his fathers'. He died on 12th March 1624 at the tender age of 2 years and 2 months, the son of Robert and Penelope. According to the inscription, little James 'frightened' his parents 'by promising too much for earth to harbour long' and it is difficult to be sure exactly what this may mean, but it goes on more confidently by referring to '.. the father of us all that owned him from his cradle and now joys in his assumption celestial.' Then it says 'Stoope dust and ashes, and let heart and voice of men and angels bless the God of Gods, which gives his grace… to rejoice gain out of loss, comfort … Adieu God's darling. Go possess that crown …'

The utterances of the bereaved are the desperate cries of those who are left behind. They may talk in riddles but their language is authentic because they are the only people who know what the separation means to them. I discovered that Robert and Penelope married later in life, she a well-connected widow from Cornwall, he a wealthy and distinguished scholar of Trinity College Cambridge, landowner, ambassador for Queen Elizabeth I to Scotland, France and Denmark, then knighted by King James; and it was he who built the great mansion by the church, planning to found a dynasty there. So this toddler, James, was the only son and heir to that aging, doting couple who once worshipped in this church with all their household.

Chapter 5
HEARTS AND MEANINGS

On Friday 16th February it was half term and I was having breakfast with three small boys, grandsons. One of them, Noah, was looking out of the window and not eating so I asked him what he was thinking about and he said straight out 'I'm wondering two things – what is the meaning of life and what are we going to be doing today?' I have always been uneasy about the first question so I played for time: 'We're going to cut and stack enough logs to keep us warm till next Christmas', I said and they all cheered. 'As for the meaning of life,' I said, 'will you give me a little time, say, till Easter?' and he agreed, but Barney was already putting his boots on in the yard. We cut the logs and I was astonished, as I always have been, by the energy and application of small people. Part of my mind that day was mulling over the answer to the other question. I felt sure that as I prepared my mardle and, in particular, contemplated the monastic system upon which that little church was founded, an answer would come to me of some sort. Besides, with the approach of Easter there would be no escape from the matter. Later in the day, when I thought back on that innocent question however, that early-morning voice 'I'm wondering two things', it occurred to me that he may not have been asking me for an answer at all. He may have been simply mentioning that he was doing what everyone does from time to time and, 'Come off it old man, nobody in his right mind expects an answer to that sort of question: it's just one of those things that people do like other animals – haven't you seen a cow standing there, doing it? Or a swallow on a telegraph wire? Or speedwell in the grass in May?' And I'm sure I would have replied, 'Oh yes, I see. You mean, nobody can answer the question but we all like to think about it sometimes in our idle moments?' and he would have said 'Exactly. Now can we get to work on those logs please?'

I do not believe he thinks there is no answer. I suspect he thinks we cannot grasp it mentally. His impatience to get on with the physical work was a child's instinctive understanding that the answer really does lie in the soil, that by wrestling with Mother Earth in all her forms we will get to know all the important answers and solutions in life. Intellectualisation and verbalisation are poor substitutes for the real thing. Don't ask a ploughman, a flint-knapper, a bricklayer, a nurse, a dancer or a chef what they believe: just look at their work and, 'By their fruits ye shall know them.'

In the course of my hospital treatment I asked a cardiology technician called Ruby about the meaning of life and she said she didn't know but the most wonderful thing she did know was the heart. Her work is to film people's hearts all day for the consultant. She showed me mine. I was fascinated by the faithful movements of those frail little valves and by the general liveliness of the whole organ which, I calculated, had beaten between two and three billion times since I was born. Ruby said that within 16 days of conception the heart alone was in perfect working order and that it was the only organ which was not fully dependent upon the brain – it 'thought' for itself, had its own nervous system, responded to all the needs of the body, all the crises, without direct reference to the brain. And, she said, with a note of triumph, 'We do not know how this happens, it remains a mystery. Imagine', she went on, 'within 16 days that tiny, perfect organ which has grown from the fusion of two minute cells starts to beat and nobody knows how.'

I tried to find out what the consultant thought about the 'mystery' of the beating heart. He was a suave man and kicked the question quickly into touch with 'I shouldn't believe everything Ruby tells you', and showed me the door. My GP was equally disappointing: 'It's not a mystery at all, it's pure organic chemistry … same in an elephant as in a shrew, except one lasts longer because it beats more slowly… and the chemicals don't get exhausted so quickly.' And I have asked many other people. They usually find it easier to describe the purpose of life than its meaning. One of my favourite replies came from a good friend, Alan Flatman, a skilled and gentle digger driver from Wilby. He said he did not know what the meaning was but he thought it had something to do with what we did and, he said, 'Heaven is all around us here already, I sometimes think.'

So I do not think the meaning of life can be experienced or expressed intellectually and I do not think these days most people, being divorced from Mother Earth, can easily experience it in their work. In spite of this I approached Noah in Easter week, trembling, and said the solution lay with the monks who built the priory and maintained it for 350 years. They sought to find a sensible balance between their prayers and their work, and the answer lay in that balance. For non-religious people it was the balance between, on the one hand, their aspirations/hopes/beliefs and, on the other, their work and the way they conducted their lives, but it was harder for them without a creed or principles to refer to.

The answer seemed ragged to me, so I was surprised when he said, 'Thank you, Grandpa. I think that is a good answer.' I felt very chuffed but wasn't entirely satisfied and continued to struggle with it because I think it's part of the reason for preserving 'such relics as Letheringham Priory Church' in healthy running order: one of the reasons people go there is, I believe, to find meaning in their lives, to get to the mysterious heart of the matter by one means or another. Further reasons were to dawn on me.

Chapter 6
THE MASS

At half past eight on the morning of Sunday 18th February there was to be a ceremony of breath-taking antiquity in the church and I set out to make it my third visit to the place. Because the church had no priest of its own at that time, a priest was coming up from Ipswich to celebrate the last meal Jesus had shared with his disciples. Elements of the ceremony dated back to the original event and had survived numerous translations, additions, omissions and debates, eventually reaching our language some 450 years ago, thanks chiefly to Thomas Cranmer, the Archbishop of Canterbury, who was burned to death in Oxford by Queen Mary for bringing it about. His English version is still used to this day in churches like Letheringham but elsewhere there is (for me) a confusion of experimental alternatives; many new bishops are encouraging this trend but I don't think it can last for too long because people will want the sturdier language and bolder theology of Cranmer and his colleagues. We shall see.

These thoughts crossed my mind as I drove over from Rendham; and the usual misgivings followed them. Am I unable to move with the times? So many people I admire use the new versions. I arrived in the field above the church and parked the car with a dozen others. I felt ashamed of my car. It is a contradiction of the faith I claim to have – that it is easier for a camel to pass through the eye of a needle than for a rich man to enter the kingdom of heaven. I should have cycled to church, or walked. It would have taken only one or two hours and I had all the time in the world that day, and I could have given the £5 spent on the car to the upkeep of the building. Some onlookers say churchgoers are hypocrites and in my case they may be right.

Now I am at the door and my wretched thoughts are dissolved by people with smiles and books and I take up residence in one of the boxed pews. A closed or boxed pew is a useful apparatus in which one can easily lie down and sleep without distracting anyone else. I decided not to do that. The priest from Ipswich swishes past in his black and white cassock and surplice with the flash of a green stole about his neck and stands with his back to us before the little altar in the east, swathed in sunlight. He stands in silence. We are kneeling before the glorious throne of heaven – there really is no other way of putting it. I have done this before at Stonehenge with eighty white-clad druids at dawn in midsummer and there is no difference – people standing, they believe, before their Maker in homage, it is the same since the world began.

Now the priest is mumbling the Lord's Prayer as if privately, preparing himself, and then he raises his arms a little and the dialogue begins. It is at this point that the unbelievers may turn away, and I do not blame them, for the silence is enough and needs no words – I remember thinking this when the talking started at Stonehenge. I think farm animals feel the same at dawn and I am sure Buddhists and Quakers do, but the more cerebral people try to address the thing in words and that, for the unbeliever, sometimes breaks the spell. However, for me, when the words are slowly and well-spoken they are magnificent: 'Almighty God, unto whom all hearts be open, all desires known and from whom no secrets are hid, cleanse the thoughts of our hearts by the inspiration of thy Holy Spirit ...'

Some outsiders find the little word 'God' too trivial for what it represents. Luckily we are not Russians whose word for God is 'Bog'. We cannot discard the word, for it is extremely primitive, pre-Christian and pre-Jewish, and it is a busy word with a double meaning combining the ideas of inviting or calling down and of offering up some gift; and of course, it was also used in the context of a sacrifice. I find all this quite reasonable but I remain in total sympathy with those who feel that the provenance of the majestic universe in which we find ourselves can only be viewed in silence, often in adoration; and they are in good company because the Jews who wrote down and copied out the original Old Testament between 900 and 500BC wrote their word for God without any vowels mainly so that no outsider would be able to read it, let alone violate it by uttering it aloud! The name to them was too wonderful for mere mortals to breathe in anything but a whispering of the soul.

I was not thinking all these things that February

morning. The ceremony is now moving on and I leave the outsiders behind. The priest turns to us and says, 'Let your light so shine before men, that they may see your good works and glorify your Father which is in heaven …' Then again later, 'Ye that do truly and earnestly repent you of your sins and are in love and charity with your neighbours, and intend to live a new life … Draw near with faith and take this Holy Sacrament to your comfort; and make your humble confession to Almighty God, meekly kneeling upon your knees …' and then follows our grovelling confession. He forgives our sins and says 'Lift up your hearts' and, turning to the east, he continues with more delight, ending with '… therefore with Angels and Archangels and in all the company of heaven, we laud and magnify thy glorious name, evermore praising thee….'

Finally there comes the feast and he says, 'We do not presume to come to this thy Table, O merciful Lord, trusting in our own righteousness …' and after the feast he concludes with these words, turning towards us: 'The peace of God which passeth all understanding, keep your hearts and minds in the knowledge and love of God and of his Son, Jesus Christ …' And away we go!

When the priory was built and for the following 350 years until the Reformation, the priest would have concluded with the Latin words '*Ite, missa est!*' meaning 'Go forth! You are dismissed!' and that incidentally is probably the origin of the word Mass, a sobriquet for the sacred feast. When the reformers booted the Roman Christians out they tore down the rood screens which separated the performing priesthood in their sanctuaries from the mute observers in their naves and destroyed much else in their churches. The serious thinkers among them had sought to commune personally with the Almighty in their midst, calling the meal a 'Communion', and shying away from the decorative and more ceremonial rites of Rome.

Today those two factions which fought each other so savagely during the period of the Reformation have, in the commemoration of that last meal about 2000 years away, moved a little closer to each other. The similarities between the reformed Church of England and the Roman Church seem close to me. But many onlookers remain dumbfounded, not only by the unseemly divisions among the churches but also by the complications of their ceremonies; and those of them who have read the Gospels wonder why the Christians today do not just meet modestly in their houses with their like-minded families and friends – the Jews still do, so did the Christians in the first couple of centuries, and if they could recover such a custom, they say, those expensive church buildings would not be needed anymore!

However, as the Great Global Collapse sets in, things will change. Food and water, along with all else, will become so scarce that we will learn again to treat such basics with respect. We will no longer confuse luxuries with necessities. Such words as snack will vanish. We will no longer die of alcohol, obesity and inertia but of malnutrition. Hunger and strife will sharpen our view of things, and each time we sit down and eat we will once again thank our lucky stars! Christians will break bread with strangers and mutter their half-remembered graces together. Old communities will re-discover a long-abandoned identity in their fields, around their hearths and at their tables and, for company and consolation, they will return to their stout churches which we have kept safely repaired for them.

There is a lively organisation called the Suffolk Historic Churches Trust which raises money for and organises the rescue and maintenance of churches like Letheringham. Its view of things to come is less histrionic than mine. One of its officers, Patrick Grieve, lives near us and he says the urgent reason for their work is to keep the churches in good trim for future generations. He says he has no doubt that as oil becomes more scarce people will have to return to work the land and become less mobile, and the churches are the only remaining visible sign of a community, without which villages will disappear. From 1790, he says, the villages emptied their folk into the industrial towns, and the time will come when they start returning to live and work in villages again. Letheringham must have been one of the last to 'empty' if *Akenfield* is anything to go by. Patrick's particular task in the Trust is to help organise the annual sponsored bike ride in September which is in effect a steeplechase and has raised £3.5m in twenty five years and this is their main source of funds – a most felicitous state of affairs in every way. Church people and sympathisers with a whole range of motives are finding the money to do the work. The next stage – and it is already happening in some places – is that they should themselves do the work, like those 'naughty monks.' The churchmongers of Letheringham say they already find as many ways as they can to do it themselves.

The diocesan office has issued a brilliant DVD showing a builder detecting examples of decay in a church which need to be dealt with early. I think churchgoers who do this sort of work would be better called churchmongers because the word suggests activity, whereas churchgoer seems more passive to me. The Letheringham people are certainly churchmongers in every way, for they do the work and finance much of the upkeep themselves. But I must not use the term too often for Polly and some of the others do not like it.

For the remainder of February I thought much about the purpose of the church in Letheringham. What do the people themselves think they are up to? When you ask such people such questions they produce a great variety of answers but apart from the most obvious ones about God and worship there is a reply that none of them gives precisely. It is, in the words of some enquiring Greek visitors to Jerusalem in about AD29, 'Sir, we would see Jesus.' Today's country people are usually hesitant to use such language because they do not want to be discarded as odd. But townies are less timid. By seeking such a relationship they believe they encounter the divine and thereby reach a happier state in their lives. I have a good friend, Rollo Wicksteed, a devout atheist, who says 'They go to church to talk to their imaginary friend!' That's the sort of remark they do not like to hear. They are rational people on the whole but going to church does imply the completely irrational assumption that Jesus of Nazareth is not dead and a rendezvous is still possible.

They believe they go to church to 'see' him in a ritualistic re-enactment of his last meal with his inner group of friends, in which they eat bread and drink wine believing, variously, that these elements are in reality his body and blood. It is a blatant simulation of human sacrifice *and* cannibalism! But, to be fair, Jesus did also tell them at that meal to do it, 'in remembrance of me', so the event has always been subjected to a wide range of interpretations. It was one of the Reformation's bitterest quarrels but the clever Archbishop Cranmer resolved it by including both aspects in the reforming church's service which was translated into a formal type of English of four hundred and fifty years ago.

The other way the people set out to 'see' Jesus today is by an unapologetic process of brainwashing. They read stories about him from the four biographies and other early writings, they sing rhymes about him and they listen to eulogies from the pulpit – which is a box on a pedestal into which the priest climbs to enhance his authority and his audibility. (Buddhists similarly ensure that the Bikkhu's head is always higher than those of his pupils.) By these means the people remind themselves of the virtues of Jesus and by a mixture of chanting and other forms of often repetitive verbalisation they bring him to mind; sometimes they say they sense his real presence – he did say, according to one report, that 'where two or three are gathered together in my name, there am I in the midst of them'.And they believe this in general terms and especially in the Mass.

So, by these means, the people set out to 'see Jesus'. They go with some humility because they know they are in need, expecting to be changed or hoping for some renewal of meaning in their lives, for insight, for inspiration and for courage. It is not like anything else they do. It is a rather unusual form of behaviour, but it has taken place in this building for eight hundred years – and most probably before that in Letheringham long, long before the Priory was built.

A friend in Laxfield, who is not a believer, says she cannot understand how Christianity has gone on for so long because, she says, 'to me it looks quite exhausted'. And about twenty-five years ago I also heard an Anglican bishop telling a hall full of teenagers that he thought the world's religions were approaching a third phase: the first had been scattered varieties of animism and pantheism; the second, which he thought was flagging, is our present age of organised religions; the third, he thought, will be some sort of amalgamated world religion. His name was David Brown, Bishop of Jordan, and then of Guildford. Perhaps this is what is beginning to happen. We shall see.

The strength of those churches which are not flagging today seems to reside in their impossible claim that Jesus rose from the dead, and they are quite sure that, inasmuch as they emerge from their churches following his way of life, he remains alive and well. They see his way as being decent chaps rather than dirty cads, to use the workaday language of my very old prep school, and in every way to do what he did: making peace, forgiving, healing, judging compassionately, giving unostentatiously, loving 'neighbours', rebelling bravely against oppression and injustice, dealing honestly, living simply, serving humbly, being grateful for small mercies, being optimistic, eschewing humbug and saying their prayers.

Churchgoers are anxious not to appear too pious, too precious about their behaviour. So it is indelicate to quiz them on this subject and they are as evasive about it as anyone would be being quizzed about their sex life. They are also secretive about it because they know so well how often they let the side down.

The technical term for the believers' extraordinary approach to life is, as they say, 'We become the Body of Christ'. For the unbeliever such idioms are acutely uncomfortable. The term Christ is the main problem. It is a concept which has existed in many faiths and long before the Christians hijacked it. The Christ word stands for the ideal person who will lead people out of the thrall of their enemies and problems to a place where they can dwell in peace. It is a romantic Jewish concept coming from the most primitive roots. I once heard a Buddhist Bikkhu exhort his pupils to be 'Christlike' and, on another occasion, he agreed with a Franciscan Friar that Nirvana was identical with the Kingdom of Heaven, that state of blissful peace which is the goal of their ambition. If the purpose of Christian churches is to bring such benefits to the human race, who can complain?

The climax of the Mass occurs when the priest puts the consecrated bread and wine into the hands of each believer and tells him or her that it is now the body and blood of the 'Lord Jesus Christ' and they must feed on him in their hearts, remember his exemplary life and be thankful. So at the very centre of that famous ritual stands Jesus the Christ, not simply Jesus the man from Nazareth.

There are quite a number of people in the world who are completely satisfied with the historical silhouette of Jesus of Nazareth in the four Gospels. Simply that, and they feel no need for the Church where Jesus the Christ reigns. Indeed they know churchgoing would upset their picture of him altogether. In their view Jesus of Nazareth was a truly marvellous person. Their picture of him is personal and their admiration as strong as anyone's who has read a good biography, for experienced readers of biographies have learnt to ignore the idiosyncrasies of authors and fillet out for themselves the substance of the characters they want to meet. I think my father-in-law, Morris Woodford, was this sort of person. He could not be doing with conversations about religion so if ever he felt threatened with one he would say, 'Well, I'm a Blue Domer', and the subject would be nervously dropped at once. Only his immediate family knew he was saying under his breath that there was nothing he loved more than going for walks with the dogs under the blue dome of heaven; the natural world thrilled him and he was particularly fascinated by birds and the reserve at Minsmere. Those walks were all the ritual he needed, together with routines like carving the Sunday joint and raising a glass to some family anniversary or to Her Majesty the Queen on Christmas Day, and going to weddings and funerals. He knew where he stood. His father had read the Bible to him and his four brothers in their young days and he often betrayed a broad knowledge of its contents. He was widely read, and much music would move him to tears. He was congenial, sociable and modest; he had natural virtues which some Christians struggle to acquire.

Because of people like my father-in-law, I think that, of the so-called outsiders who are impressed by the character of Jesus, very many mean usually Jesus of Nazareth, the young Jew a long time ago who went about preaching a rare wisdom and doing good, and was wrongly executed. And I think the Reformation and many other reforming movements have sought to simplify things and get back, to some extent, to the original historical Jesus – movements as diverse as Monasticism in third-century Egypt and Quakerism in seventeenth-century Leicestershire.

John Brentnall, the theological Beachcomber of Walberswick twenty miles up the coast, believes that if people were able to come face to face with the original man Jesus they would be surprised. For even the earliest documents are lensed through their authors' outlooks, and nothing we have was written in the Syrian language which Jesus spoke. Moreover, while he yet lived, Jesus is reported to have been constantly misunderstood – the film *Life of Brian* illustrates the effect well: 'I think it was "Blessed are the cheesemakers".' 'What's so special about the cheesemakers?' And a furious argument ensues so that the Preacher is no longer heard.

Furthermore, very many of his sayings are to be found in the ancient Jewish scriptures – not surprising if he was a rabbi, but it makes you wonder how much of what he is reported to have said were his own original words; or do we find we are merely admiring – heaven forbid! – the teaching and personality of a brilliant and typical Jew?

Somewhere between the earthly life of that man and the present day, he has become enshrined within a complex, theological structure and rebranded 'Jesus the Christ'. It started during his lifetime, some recognising in him the Messianic quality they had longed for and many imposing their own variations on that theme. Again, *Life of Brian* illustrates the confusion well, but so do the fans of Elvis Presley or Marilyn Monroe as they make their heroes into what they want them to be.

It is interesting that the four New Testament biographers used the Christ word sparingly compared with St Paul, that exuberant, brainy convert whose use of splendid Christly titles was eleven times more frequent than his use of the plain name Jesus. He made no bones about it – his lord and master was 'Jesus the Christ', risen, glorious, triumphant, powerful, supreme and everlasting.

And so from there, the theological carnival swept gaily along for three hundred years gathering in variety and extravagance until the Emperor Theodosius decided it had gone too far: for his purposes of unifying and controlling the (now so-called 'Christian') state, one expression of belief must be selected and made law; promotion of any other would become a crime.

It is at the juncture where Jesus the historical man from Nazareth merges with that Utopian figure of Jesus the Christ that people like my father-in-law quietly leave the party. Others choose to stay, some rushing ahead with Pauline fervour but most, I reckon, quietly turning up hoping to encounter the divine through that mysterious merger.

When the Greeks in AD29 said they wanted to 'see Jesus' they were not given an interview but were told indirectly that they could get the most explicit picture of him at his death, which was imminent. This shaft of insight is found in the biography written by an old man in Turkey in about AD90 who had not himself met Jesus but probably heard about him from St John, the 'disciple whom Jesus loved'. The other three biographers – Matthew, Mark and Luke – who had written much closer to the event, observed the same thing but more subtly: they all recorded that, as Jesus began his journey up to Jerusalem to meet his death, a blind man begged for his sight back and, when Jesus opened the man's eyes, he followed him gleefully all the way to the end. Thus, according to the earliest records available, the secret of all that Jesus of Nazareth did and said is, we are told, to be found in the manner of his death, and churchgoers seek their communion with the divine by celebrating that event. It may seem a macabre habit to the onlooker yet it is a commonplace to theatregoers who also mysteriously enjoy much refreshment from the cathartic effect of a well-told tragedy. At each celebration of this particular tragedy, Jesus of Nazareth becomes one with the resplendent Utopian Christ, and the participants themselves leave their churches, as the Bikkhu bid, a little more Christ-like than before.

It is now about half past nine on that February morning as we emerge from our little celebration at Letheringham, prattling away in twos and threes through the south porch and into the graveyard, strangely invigorated as always, and on this occasion spurred by the chilly air. The only onlookers are a small covey of French partridges on the Gatehouse wall who tut-tut a little and then fly off cackling with laughter.

Chapter 7
IMAGINARY FRIENDS

Rollo's remark about 'their imaginary friend' troubled me and early on the following Tuesday I went back to the church to do some thinking. Queen Victoria recorded one day in her diary of 1875 that she had sought to console some of the mourners at a Highland funeral by saying, among other things, that the Church made one think of what one would not otherwise think of. Surely I could do no better than heed the words of this former Supreme Governor of the Church of England?

At the gate I stood, looking across the gravestones at its mute form framed in a wide wet welkin, heard the dew drip heavily from thin springy trees, felt the metal of the latch, breathed deeply the young day's honest air. May I enter?

Passing between the tombs and the grasses I heard an old horse blowing his nose on the other side of the wall and an eager van humming along the lane from Hoo beyond the church. Two dark velvet jackdaws dived away down from the tower without speaking. At the outer door of the porch there was no one to greet me – what did I expect?

Through the porch and inside the church I was no stranger for I already knew its emptiness and felt safely at home there. I stopped in the aisle, where I had previously chatted happily with fellow churchgoers, now alone and unattended. If I were the last man on earth, who would I be? I would not need a name and, if there were no other people left here to know me, would I exist? And if I were the only astronaut aboard a mis-directed spacecraft hurtling away from Earth with, say, a fortnight's rations and no radio contact, what visions and insights might penetrate my frail perception in those last days? Would the meaning of life, existence and consciousness at last dawn on me? But if it did, how would I tell Noah and his brethren? Or would it be too marvellous to be communicated? Having received it in full, could it only be passed on in part? This is how I felt that morning in that lovely place and the ensuing thoughts excited me much.

Did whoever killed the last bear out there in England know it was the last bear? And was his crime recorded anywhere? And has anyone ever read about it? If it is neither written of nor read about, how do we know that it happened? Or that bears ever existed? If no one remembers things, did they really happen?

I still have my own teddy bear. His name is Rupert, a matchless moniker and a matchless friend and brother since my first year on Earth. Is he a worthy representative of those creatures who roamed our former forests outside? To me he is more real than they, for he faithfully awaits my return each day, sitting by my empty bed with drooping open arms and battered countenance, knowing everything that has happened to me in the past seventy-odd years and, his body language tells me, emanating approval. Rupert is a real friend, not imaginary. I know he ranks among the dolls but I do not worship him so I cannot be accused of idolatry. I have projected onto him over the years some of the human qualities which I admire: patience, equanimity, quiet wisdom, modesty, politeness, good looks, a sense of humour, courage, a taste for adventure and a respect for fair play ... and he used to have a deep, furry voice which I regarded as very masculine. I envied him because mine was never deep. His faded away quite early on but I can still clearly remember it. Although he has been dumb for many years he still looks at me in a way which says, 'You know very well what I think, dear boy', and I do, because he thinks invariably those admirable thoughts that I have projected onto him. So he is also my self-appointed judge and he is a merciful, avuncular judge.

My thoughts wander among these sorts of things from time to time. They are like those of a child talking to its toys. Am I mad? The newspaper yesterday reported that psychologists in La Trobe University, Australia believe that children aged between three and nine with 'personified toys' were not loners but 'highly interactive and creative people' because they have to 'invent both sides of the conversation'. When questioned about such conversations, the children chide them, they say, with remarks like, 'It's not true, you know. It's only pretend.' I would like to ask these researchers what they make of children aged between thirty and ninety who converse with their cars, golf balls, photographs of loved ones, wooden legs, bread (while it rises), dogs and cats, trees and flowers.

And my father-in-law had a memorable story about a policeman giving evidence in a magistrate's court in about 1930 which went like this: 'Yes, Your Honour, the accused was sitting on the park bench and he had exposed his person and placed his spectacles upon his person and was addressing it in this manner: 'Have a good look round, it's your birthday, you can have what you fancy.' We all laughed louder than usual hoping, I expect, that others would note our surprise to hear that such a trifling offence could exist in the catalogue of human folly. Yet, according to books like *Lady Chatterley's Lover*, to regard that organ as an intelligent personage is not uncommon between couples. It is their go-between, the third person in the marriage, without whom they could not do. The thought rang a bell somewhere ... something to do with the function of three, and it was to crop up again a fortnight later.

Thus I stood in the aisle thinking about my teddy bear and things – not exactly what Her Late Majesty might have expected perhaps – and I began to wonder why I had come. I may have been hoping to find a picture or at least a symbol of some sort, but I already knew there were none for they had all been swep' away in the Reformation. I knew that one or two gravestones bore Christian emblems but inside the church there was nothing of the sort. At the back there are the remains of carved stones rescued from various local sites and now displayed in fine oak cabinets.

And there is a lively little organ built by Roger Pulham of Charsfield in 1984 and donated by Mary Wood in 1991 with leaves and musical instruments carved into its oaken frame. And, painted on wood above the south door where I entered, a delightfully human-looking lion with a unicorn calls down shame in antiquated French upon anyone who dares to think evil of others. And there are one or two plaques and brasses dedicated to the memory of various dead people. But this hollow, hallowed house contains no images whatsoever of its Lord and Master, nor of his mother Mary to whose protection its builders dedicated their work, let alone of The Almighty himself and his 'Holy Spirit'. Strange.

I sighed and took a final glance to the east, then realised that a large brass cross stood on the little altar, a familiar symbol easily overlooked. Reluctantly I agreed that it did represent the Man long gone. But it bore no crucified figure upon it so, surely, it symbolises an idea rather than a person. As I approach, it occurs to me that the cross is empty because the victim's body has been removed and, his disciples might remind me, after burial he was raised from the dead, so a symbol of their risen Lord is more appropriate than a lifelike crucifix would be in that position.

I reach the altar rail and peer across at the well-proportioned, well-polished metal of the cross and am confronted suddenly by a reflection of my own disgruntled face. My laughter rebounds from the tower behind and I turn quickly to make sure no one else has come into the church.

To my right, a lectern bears a great old Bible; so I step up and open it, smelling its thick worn paper and warming to its bold lettering. This book of course (I scold myself) contains imagery more intimate than contemporary craftsmanship can devise. The big book falls open at a scene in about 1000BC in which the king-to-be David agonises over two close friends killed in battle. It is a famous and moving passage. I read several chapters of his exploits and then skip on a chunk of pages to where Psalm number 139 confronts me from about the same time chanting about the nature of the Almighty: '... thou hast searched me out and known me, thou knowest my thoughts long before... thou art about my path and about my bed ... thou hast fashioned me behind and before and laid thine hand upon me. Such knowledge is too wonderful and excellent for me, I cannot attain unto it... if I take the wings of the morning and remain in the uttermost parts of the sea, even there also shall thy hand lead me, and thy right hand shall hold me... the darkness is no darkness with thee ... For my reins are thine, thou hast covered me in my mother's womb. I will give thanks unto thee, for I am fearfully and wonderfully made. Marvellous are thy works, and that my soul knoweth right well.'

This is three-thousand-year-old poetry and now I am shouting aloud, howling and sobbing, as I proclaim these fabulous images to a vast host, a field full of folk as far as the eye can see. The windows shatter and the crowded hills heave with their approval as they emerge from the fields and the forests above, gathering like windswept clouds of thunder, expectantly. As I watch, they remove their hats and bow their heads, a mighty throng braced for the moment of recognition. For they all know that the fantastic majesty of this universe in which we find ourselves cannot adequately be described by people except in their poetry, their music and dancing. We may have gasped with incomprehension at the revelations of Galileo Galilei, Charles Darwin and David Attenborough but we can only grasp the beauty of their science through the eyes of the poet that is within each of us.

So I turn over another chunk of pages and there stands the prophet Micah in about 750BC, a countryman with typical misgivings about town-dwellers, rich property owners, government orders and weak-willed priests. He had a red-hot social conscience and fearlessly condemned the expropriation of smallholders from their properties and peasants from their land, all of which had become widespread since the time of Ahab. He also condemned child-slavery, money-grubbers and promotion-conscious prophets. To him the Holy City of Jerusalem was a sick joke. And living as he did near the Gaza frontier he was also more aware of the dangers of foreign powers to a weakened state than were the ruling classes in Jerusalem. Like the other prophets, he foresaw the coming of a 'Messiah', by which he meant a David-like hero and brave military deliverer who would bring peace and justice far and wide.

The people who have gathered outside now seem to like what they hear and are reduced to complete silence as I come to the last sentences: 'Hear ye now what the Lord saith! ... The Lord's voice crieth unto the city ... What doth the Lord require of thee? ... to do justice, to love mercy and to walk humbly with thy God.' I look up, my eyes showing affirmation of what is on their faces: 'Yes, yes!' we cry out together and again, all throwing our hats in the air, 'Oh yea!'

I am getting weary now and fumble through the last chunk of pages to where St Matthew, the utter Jew in Syria somewhere between AD50 and 85, was quoting from the sayings of Jesus of Nazareth whom he himself had never met. I wonder if he regarded him as his imaginary friend. He certainly believed he was their long-awaited Messiah. That may be a state of mind which is beyond the comprehension of non-believers today, yet most people find no difficulty in accepting at least in theory the wisdom of his famous words in these passages which I start to read. Jesus, the travelling rabbi, is talking to the country people up north in those early, halcyon days among the flowery hills of Galilee between about AD27 and 29.

My London daughter, Lucy, once arranged for me to visit, among other middle-Eastern places, Capernaum which overlooks the northern coast of the Sea of Galilee, and there by the water I listened to a young girl reading to a crowd of tourists from these very passages. Such was the purity of her voice and the tranquillity of the place, that I was bodily transported to the original event, or so I believed. Of course, I only imagined I was there but the intensity of the experience was every bit as tremendous as any other I have known in so-called real life. And of course, this is nothing unusual, as every theatregoer knows.

Some of the crowd have now come into the church and they fill every corner, every sill. They do not mind the lengthiness of it and each time I pause some of them shout 'More! More!' These are some of the sayings I am reading aloud on this bright Suffolk morning. Get rid of your possessions. Give to the poor, only do it secretly, so secretly that you 'let not thy left hand know what thy right hand doeth'. Do some fasting, also secretly: 'anoint thine head and wash thy face ... appear not unto men to fast, but unto thy Father which is in secret.' Pray alone. Don't fret about food and clothes and what you are going to do tomorrow – be like the birds and the flowers 'for the morrow will take heed of the things of itself'.

Be pure in heart. Be meek. Don't criticise. Make peace. 'Bless them that curse you.' 'Love your enemies, do good to them which hate you.' Be like a child. By such means you should seek the bliss of the Kingdom of Heaven, here and now, becoming 'the salt of the earth' and light in a dark place: 'Let your light so shine before men that they may see your good works and glorify [not you but] your Father which is in Heaven.'

To my crowd that Tuesday morning I was reading from the big old Authorised Version of the Bible, officially published in 1611, as ordered by King James I. It had been largely derived from the first translation of

William Tyndale, a young Gloucestershire scholar hiding from Queen Mary in Hamburg, whose straightforward, vigorous work was edited and published by a lovely Birmingham man educated at Cambridge who then smuggled it to England, disguising it under the title 'Matthew's Bible', and was eventually burnt by Queen Mary at Smithfield for his defiance of Rome in 1555. That publisher was a man of admirable fortitude, incidentally, for the French ambassador who was present at the burning recorded that he had approached his death with the composure of a bridegroom going to his wedding. Tyndale himself had been strangled and burnt near Brussels in 1536 at the tender age of 42. Since those dire times, this very book spread throughout the world wherever English was spoken for the next three centuries and the power of its language has remained unchallenged by other translations until the last hundred years. Victor Hugo, a hundred years ago, thought that England had 'two books, the Bible and Shakespeare; England made Shakespeare but the Bible made England' he said. The compliment was referring to this very edition of which the Parish of Letheringham keeps a copy on the lectern of its church.

(The passages above from Psalm 139 however have been taken from a later version of Tyndale's Bible composed by Miles Coverdale who added his own Latin mind to that of Tyndale's translation from the Greek and Hebrew. Coverdale's phrasing can be chanted well in places of worship and this may be why Cranmer preferred to use his psalms in the Book of Common Prayer for the daily use of the reforming Church in England.)

I closed the book and looked up. They were smiling all round and murmuring among themselves. They began to leave, some singing as they went, looking much like today's people. I blinked, and they were gone. I ambled down the aisle. The door was heavy, I had had no breakfast, my chest ached and I was feeling weak again, so outside I sat in the grass on my raincoat and found I was next to the small grave of Robert Villiers Dove, not far from the porch. He had died just before reaching his seventh birthday in July 1874 and his distraught parents had carved the monogram IHS into the headstone, meaning more or less, 'Jesus we have as our companion.' That Jesuit interpretation, I thought, was a sweet representation of the Man from Nazareth. A companion? It was enough for me. I looked sentimentally on the grave by my side, with its wrought iron nursery fencing and its mantle of last year's trefoils and fescues. Not yet seven, still in heaven, and what a name! The tragedy dragged me down for a while.

By and by I stood up and started home, my spirits much refreshed by the morning's work. It had been thoughtless of me to have reacted against Rollo's jibe, for what way other than in the imagination can the mind process friendships? Certainly not in the rational department since it is too controlling for friendship. And memory is reserved for the dead. But imagination is the creature of the future, of adventure, optimism and love.

Chapter 8
THE LAND

Friday 2nd March. When Roger Keene the architect offered to take me up the tower of course I accepted at once and we went there and then, he with a big old key and I, as we approached the door, with a little trepidation. We corkscrewed our way up the cold stone stair, conversation was scant and in the dim light I knew I was less fit than I used to be. I do not know why people built towers and spires onto churches. I have heard all the theories and I wonder whether the strongest motive was usually a sort of bravado. There are some 740 towers in Suffolk, mainly built between 1300 and 1500, and usually added to existing churches. This tower was quite an early one and is a modest but handsome specimen. The stairway ends at the level of the nave's roof, into whose darkness I now breathlessly peered. With a torch I could see its length and its simple reconstruction of 1790, when several of its timbers looked as if they had been salvaged from the old roof.

(What I could not see on this occasion was that the top angle of the roof at the far end above the altar was wider than its angle this end above my head. In fact I did not notice it until a long time after when I saw it in Lucy's illustration for the cover of this book. It means that the ridge slopes downhill about two feet to the altar end, but the gutters are level, and so the tiled roof twists gently on both sides. I still find it hard to see this from the ground outside because I do not have the practised eye of an artist. It seems important to mention this because it demonstrates the unreliability of our precious perceptions. We like to think we see things as they really are but in fact we cannot be relied upon always to do so.

The sharp western angle, incidentally, indicates a probability that the roof had been thatched prior to 1800, but why the contractor then widened the angle in the east is inexplicable.)

A pause for breath. The second part of the ascent was to be up a wooden ladder and here I discovered that I was less brave than I used to be. I could not turn back now because Roger, who was six years older than I, went up like a lamplighter and I feebly followed on the rattling rungs. Halfway up, he strode across onto the bell frame to demonstrate for my benefit the sweet tone of their four-hundred-year-old tenor. It was truly sweet and calmed my fears a little.

Through a hatch at the top, the blue sky, warm sun, a breath of living air and a fantastic view in all directions. Roger leaned back on the parapet, smiling like the artist showing his work. At each corner of the tower was a strange animal, carved in stone, looking outwards on guard. The nave looked much bigger from up here and I glimpsed the scale of the priory as it must have developed over its 350 years: from the gatehouse in the west, the fishponds in the north, the older barns in the east and the present yard wall in the south, it must have covered about three acres. Perhaps we can find a man with an aeroplane to photograph it at dusk or daybreak, and perhaps the bumps will reveal more. Google is not much help.

On the roof of the tower someone called J E Malins has cut his name and dated it 31st October 1878, enclosing it within the outline of a boot print. Whose boot? Who was he? To whom was he talking? If he had had time to look at the view after leaving his mark on the deck he might have spied Easton church above Pound Cottages and, if he was really keen, Kettleburgh church over a mile away to the north and, on this side of the river, Hoo church nearly a mile away, but Monewden church upstream in the west would probably have still been hidden among the trees a hundred years ago. Perhaps he has autographed some of those as well. But the main features visible from this tower today are the small woods and copses which are remnants of the ancient forest to the south in this parish and, across the river, the three main woods in Easton and, nearly two miles away in the east, the Great Wood of Glevering.

Looking down at the immediate farmstead with its medieval barns and modern machinery, at the empty almshouses higher up and, further up still, the site of the so-called 'Abbey' mansion and, round to the west, at the assumed site of the earlier Priory, I got a strong feeling that this whole area surrounding the church – an area of ten or twelve acres – had had a long history of human habitation. But I admit this could have been wishful thinking, for who am I to say? And what does it matter who lived here centuries ago? I cannot quite put my finger on why their lives should seem to affect today's people who live around here and occasionally nod into church.

The Gatehouse, thought to have been built in about 1500, is now a forlorn relic of that prosperous time. The outer walls of the Priory's perimeter and all the buildings within are gone, so it stands alone in sad purposelessness. Until then presumably there had been no need for it but when the troubled rumblings of the Reformation started, the monks needed to prevent odd people with odd ideas from disturbing their peace, reducing their cashflow, their authority and their good works. It may have been a rebuild, for most such communities set out with a gatehouse but, whichever it was, they built this one with limited success because within only twenty five years that colourful thug, King Henry VIII of England, was to dissolve the mother house in Ipswich and, in a further ten years, his Captain of the Guard (our Sir Anthony Wingfield) was to preside over the same fate for little Letheringham. King Henry with cronies like Wingfield did a sort of Bush and Blair on monasticism, destroying or pillaging every form of 'popishness', crippling its scholarship, its hospitals and its thriving tourist industry. Like them, he was of course after wealth but proceeded so clumsily that he destroyed the mechanism which was generating it. He claimed the moral high ground with ease by exploiting the great waves of intellectual (and therefore theological) disaffection for the Roman Church in England and throughout Europe. Reformers led the way intellectually and idealistically but they were accompanied by waves of commercial blokes with big white vans, by a mixture of professional house-breakers and fanatical nut-cases, and the job was finished quite quickly by the rabble who reduced what was left to rubble. Just stand in the middle of the great ruined abbey in Bury St Edmunds to feel the scale of the disaster.

So our little priory at Letheringham was stripped of all her ornaments by people with very mixed motives and finally in 1610 it was burned and the materials removed by thieving hands. I looked down from my tower and I could imagine, after the destruction, the new ministers in their severe black and white robes now entering the eastern chancel beyond our nave and the people filing in, as before, from the west beneath our feet, and they all soberly read their scriptures together, 'meekly kneeling upon their knees', and following a form of service which had been partly translated from the ancient Latin of the Roman Church and carefully re-couched by Archbishop Cranmer and company in about 1550, wishing to recover the less cluttered theology of the early church as described in the New Testament. I heard their newly-disciplined voices reciting those primitive prayers in English for the first time, prompted by their pious 'Clerk in Holy Orders'. I could no longer hear the chanting of the monks whom they had replaced. The monks, I supposed, may have fled into the countryside, labouring in rueful silence to the end of their days. But some of them, and some of the landowners, were discreetly making the doctrinal switch and becoming priests and collaborators in the reforming church. What confusion it must have been for one and all. They must have wondered from day to day where they stood, what was the right way to think and what were the latest political correctnesses. A century of bloodshed and inquietude followed.

The only Roman Catholic I know connected with Letheringham today is Peter the grass cutter. I was to meet him a fortnight later. He came with his dog and talked quietly of the peace of the place that drew him there. He was once a soldier, now a teacher of mathematics in Woodbridge and he is fascinated by the shapes to be found in ancient places of worship, their geometry and the unwritten wisdom of such concepts as irrational numbers. He comes just to be here alone in silence. I suspect many people do.

We do not know how the Priory came to be burned in 1610, but we do know that a great mansion was built by Sir Robert Naunton nearby in the following decade. It was the fourth largest house in Suffolk, a fine building with an E-shaped ground plan facing east, large bay windows and huge chimneys. It was not unlike Christchurch Mansion in Ipswich today. Sir Robert with Lady Penelope had hardly moved up from The Hall when little James, their son and heir, died. So when Sir Robert died ten years later his inheritance went sideways to brothers and nephews who were no good at producing heirs or maintaining mansions. Within seventy-five years it had to be extensively repaired and, I think, it must have been then that, when the porch was added to the church (in the same style as the mansion's renovated gables), the floor of the church was also raised some four feet above its original level – look inside at the arch in the north wall opposite, and then outside at the west door in the tower – and at the same time it looks as if the whole graveyard was levelled with the meadow to the south (which became orchards and gardens), and raised above the old priory field in the north and enclosed by the walls which retain it still today. The present concrete path from the porch, if projected southwards, would have led directly to the north door of the mansion eighty yards away, and made a stately approach to the church for his lordship with his family; everyone else would have entered through the west door beneath the tower.

I lifted up mine eyes from this holy place and looked unto the hill in the south, to the land from which this priory grew. I saw the uneasy clump called Cutters Grove, the last remnant of a woodland which had been husbanded at about this time by a family named Curtis. When the priory was built, all the land before me and beyond my view down to Potsford Brook was woodland. It stretched from the brow east of Park Farm across our skyline right over into Charsfield, Monewden and Hoo to the right towards the sources of the river Deben in the west – *Akenfield* country. Today we can only see fragments of it here and there, spared by the tree-fellers in their mercy during the last hundred years: Smiley Wood, Cutters Grove and Old Park Wood. There is a hesitant patchwork of fields, some little and very old being the lawns and closes of former forest, others bigger where our farmers today have stitched the little ones together in their valiant struggle to make a living from an unpredictable agricultural industry.

I look harder. The fields are still sullen in winter greens but the hedges look slightly more hopeful of spring. It is a hazy, sunny day and the air is fresh after night rain. I think I am seeing clearly but what I am looking at is dull. Perhaps if I had been cultivating some of those fields myself for a few years they would excite me more. There are some isolated rooftops but the land seems uninhabited to me, no stock in the fields, no hedgers and ditchers with their winter bonfires and no folk. No visible movement. I blink, but it makes no difference.

Only a quarter of the parish is visible from this tower, maybe less. Most of the cottages as well as the famous Hall and the Watermill are clustered along the river, now screened behind alders and cricket-bat willows down in the east but you can see from here the remains of the old road to Wickham Market, now a footpath faithfully left uncultivated, running alongside the seven-acre triangle of 'Fairfield' to the left which was the medieval site of their annual fair, granted its charter in 1379 at about the same time as this tower was erected, probably the most prosperous period in the village's history. The road came from Hoo, Monewden and Cretingham holding to the drier, higher ground south of the river. In the winter months it probably passed above the church as indicated by the Fairfield footpath where it continues to the west.

The granting of a charter was usually connected to a church's patronage so, in Letheringham, this might have been on the Feast of the Annunciation in March, but we do not know, and medieval fairs could then last for days or weeks thereafter.

The rest of the parish mainly lies out of sight on the southern slopes together with its half dozen farmsteads which originated in woodland clearings. Along the waterways the soils are sandy and loamy as one would expect and there are marshes and fens, carres and warrens, where the river once raced after the end of the last ice age, between about 10,000 and 7,000BC. The melting of the ice gouged out the English Channel and caused raging torrents throughout the new land from its heights down to the sea which, over the following few thousand years, finally led to the calm, meandering waters of our own era which enthralled John Constable with his paints, among many other local artists.

The types of trees that have been growing in this land since the last ice age are called our native trees today, and these types number about thirty-five. They are superior to all later imports and hybrids, generally speaking, because by the natural selection of our geology and climate they have learnt to thrive in health, longevity and quality of timber. The same goes for our native flora and fauna, but I know less about them.

I would like to know more of the peoples who migrated to this land as the ice and floods subsided. Nothing is written. One imagines sparse vegetation, then scrub, then wildwood gradually inhabited by nomadic peoples who hunted and paused in the clearings then moved on. The time came when some of them lingered and penned animals, grew things and settled. The earliest trading brought peoples from other cultures from across southern Europe and the Middle East and even India. A few of them settled and the result was a mixed race and an amalgamation of foreign cultures, both Aryan and Semite.

In the thousand years before the Christians some clearer shapes appeared. I am fascinated to learn from a German scholar, Ulrich Stutz, that parishes were a Teutonic innovation. The Teutons from Denmark held that landowners were obliged to safeguard the spiritual welfare of their people and, as necessary, appoint and maintain a priest. Christianity in this land found this structure convenient and made use of it until, alas, the Industrial Revolution when it allowed the custom to erode and the patronage of many parish livings fell into the hands of people less acquainted with the land. But what an achievement it was in those pre-Christian centuries to set up a system which lasted so effectively and for so long. The Teutons are thought to have been a division of the Celtic peoples. They were annihilated by the Romans in 102BC, for it was the habit of those ambitious invaders across Europe to deal thus with peoples they could not understand or control.

One of the patrons of the church at Letheringham today is a charity called the Church Pastoral Aid Society which was set up in 1836 by Lord Shaftesbury, among others, 'to carry the Gospel to every man's door'. According to the person I spoke to on the telephone it is now called 'The Evangelical Anglican Mission Agency' with headquarters in Warwick, a nice place but rather a long way away. Such organisations were the unavoidable result of eager Christians trying to cater for the huge migration of country folk into the industrial cities. It used to send a representative to the interviews of priests applying for livings under its jurisdiction, who 'advised' the bishop's representative on his or her 'suitability' for the parish, and helped to furnish him with a 'parish profile' for the purpose. These particular patrons, because of their favoured churchmanship, tend to look for a Low Church candidate rather than a High Church one. Today some such 'patrons' hardly exist as mortals with flesh and bones or passionate and personal interests in a parish; they are little more than bureaucratic cyphers.

In Letheringham the patronage after the de Boviles, the Wingfields and the Nauntons seems to have evaporated until it slid into the hands of the Hamiltons who came to Easton from the Isle of Arran in 1830 and departed a hundred years later. If they had been more interested they might have passed the Letheringham patronage on to local landowners like the Clarkes or the Kerrs who would have looked after it, being of farming stock and well involved with the people of the village.

Gradually over the next few months I was to discover that reaching back into the past is no easy matter and, for the amateur, doing it well is probably impossible. I began to question why I wanted to do it. On the one hand I felt I was meddling and should desist. On the other there was a strong curiosity which, I hoped, might lead to discoveries unimagined. My inhibitions dissolved however when the Kerrs allowed me to take a Norfolk enthusiast, Al Matthewson, with a metal detector outside the immediate land around the church and beyond the area of the 'scheduled ancient monument' supervised by English Heritage who allow strictly no digging. We spent a day to the west of the old path from the Gatehouse towards Charsfield. We found one Roman coin with oyster shells, and some shards which may be Roman or Saxon, we could not tell. We also found two eighteenth-century musket balls and several buttons, buckles and other modern debris, all of which are now in the hands of the PCC. At Easton Farm Park they had an earlier display of local finds from both parishes ranging from Bronze Age flints to Roman coins, clasps and brooches of AD250-350; Saxon pottery, Tudor buckles, a seventeenth-century rowel, eighteenth-century sheep's bells and loom weights, and a charming, dented nineteenth-century thimble. So it was to become clear to me that there had been a lot going on around this place for two or three thousand years but, if the flints really are Bronze Age, that goes back even further.

After the metal detecting, I was also allowed to invite a

number of East Anglian Dowsers to see what they could locate of the former Priory buildings north and west of the tower, but their findings that day were at variance with one another. Only the outline of an earlier church, close to this one, with an apothecary next to it showed any convincing concord among them. An older man from Castle Hedingham said he was sure there had been a settlement here for as long ago as three thousand years. He had never been here before but he spoke with quiet confidence of an area of about ten acres, and I had no reason to ignore him, especially after I had later plotted and drawn his findings on a map. But the day ended and I saw him no more.

I studied a recent geological survey of the church area made for the district council by very modern technicians with sonar equipment but the shapes of the 'features' on their map were ill-defined and I found their written report incomprehensible.

I also spent two days with a local dowser in the high land surrounding Letheringham Lodge and the Haugh where we found and plotted many lines of energy but could not interpret their overall significance. We had been given permission to do this by two of the landowners up there who had expressed much interest but, I am afraid, were to be disappointed. However, down in a field not far from the Mill, Paul Clarke had allowed us to investigate the rumour of a 'Saxon church' and that produced an astonishing result: a structure of about seventy-five square yards on the ground with an eastern altar, orientated exactly like the Priory Church which is 14° south of due east, but lozenge-shaped with an eastern vertex of 84° which is within one degree of Uriel's Machine at our latitude. (At Hadrian's Wall this vertex is 90° and in the northern isles of Scotland it is 108° while down at the pyramids of Giza it is only 55°, but all that is another story and not yet within the scope of my understanding. It concerns solar angles found in various stone structures of about 3000 BC and suggests a connection between the peoples who made them.)

I had gone into this venture with an open mind like a well-disciplined lab assistant, at every move obedient to what I saw before me. I had followed the dowser silently and was led to a place where a rough shape emerged. As I followed I marked out with flints each couple of steps. At the time I could not see much sense in the shape but the following day I returned alone, measured it out flint by flint and plotted it faithfully on paper. My emotions had so far slept, but now I became enthralled by the angles emerging from that silent field. The dowser had said the structure had been there 'between about AD300 and 600' and was 'probably made of wood'. I remembered that the king who is thought to have been buried at Sutton Hoo in about AD600 had kept a 'temple' dedicated to not only his Pagan gods but also the Christian one. And that particular farming settlement goes back to the Stone Age, and is only twelve miles downstream as the fish swims.

If any credence can be given to this sort of geomancy our conclusion has to be that we may have detected signs of yet one more Anglo-Saxon settlement on the banks of the River Deben. That is all. It does not tell us what they thought or believed, or what motivated their astonishing craftsmanship and wellbeing over and above the basic task of survival. Sutton Hoo provides a wondrous spectacle of such a settlement but even that is limited in explanations. In reaching back into the past, one answered question spawns a shoal of new questions. I wonder, for example, what the relationship would have been between this Mill site and the pre-Priory site a mile upstream where the present church stands. And if indeed they were Christian settlements, what sort of Jesus would they have had in mind? Would it have been the original North-country 'Jesus of Nazareth'? Or St Paul's 'Jesus Christ Our Lord'? Or would the Nicaean Jesus, 'The Very God' of Rome, have reached Letheringham yet? I would like to be at a meeting between those first Christians of Letheringham and today's church people; imagine the whoops of joy and laughter! What a meeting that would be! And afterwards we might come away knowing what had been going on here in those very early days which allowed the novelty of Christianity to take root. We know roughly what the message was but the seedbed contains half the secret of a good crop.

Having unearthed so little of the past, however, I returned to my original quandary: what makes us curious about the past? I cannot understand it, for there is as much satisfaction from discovering that we have crept out of some dismal slum as from hearing that we are descended from a celebrated dynasty. I looked down again at the tiled spine of the sleeping church beneath. Despite her mature beauty, her eight hundred years is less than half way back to the Jesus Event. Beyond the time when she was built, the sea of ignorance is very wide indeed. Then I recalled the message in the visitors' book in the church below, from a friend of Rebecca Rice: 'You are just a thought away', so the sea became navigable to me.

When William Blake, two hundred years ago, wrote about 'those feet in ancient time' walking upon our 'mountains green', what was he asking? And when Ali Bridges, a young man of Suffolk, suddenly said last year as he stood in the graveyard below, 'Do you think Jesus hung out with the druids in his hippy years?' was he offering a possible reply? Did the original Jesus of history really come to these islands before Christianity was born (that is, during the twenty hidden years between about AD5 and 25)? And, if he did, where did he go, and why? If Blake, who was deeply interested in the possibility, was right about the mountains green, it would not have been Suffolk, it must have been Wales or Scotland, or maybe Ireland. So Letheringham may not have been linked with that particular dream. Yet we do know there were druids in these parts among the Celts, for the Romans blamed Boudicca's savagery on her druids when she sacked Colchester in AD60. There is other evidence, though it is frail and slighted by mainstream historians whose sources have been mainly Roman, that some of the exiled Jews of 700BC who were kidnapped by the Babylonians may have turned left when the others turned right, and fetched up in Brittany and parts of Britain; this breakaway group, unlike the majority who went east, chose not to commit their wisdom to writing but to continue to pass it on orally as their forbears had done – and as druids are reported always to have done. This is a delicious rumour. Its proponents claim that the terms Judaism and Druidism are etymologically similar, to say nothing of their philosophies. Caesar thought that what he called 'the discipline of the druids' started in Britain but mainstream historians question this. Certainly the Roman contempt for Druids in Western Europe was only matched by their contempt for the Jews in the East! I enjoy the rumour because it makes the Blake-and-Bridges idea more palatable: if indeed Jesus spent some of his hidden years preparing for his ministry as a travelling rabbi by living with the famously wise people of somewhere like Glastonbury or Anglesea, it would explain several of the flavours of his early life and teaching up north in Galilee.

The spin doctors of Roman history only saw badness in druidism because they did not understand it and feared its power among the Celtic peoples whom J Caesar and Co. wished to subdue. A parody of the relationship comes across well in Goscinny and Uderzo's *Asterix*. Roman prejudice against the 'Gauls', as they called some of them, reinforced by the Venerable Bede's luscus history, has become an indelible ingredient in today's folklore. But some modern scholarship is finding a fairer assessment.

For most of the five centuries before the Jesus Event,

Celtic peoples had entrusted the education of their young to druids and seers who taught them the movements of the heavenly bodies and the greatness of our earth, plus natural and moral philosophy and, above all, the immortality of the soul. There was nothing in their basic teaching that could have been offensive to the earliest forms of Christianity. Hence the sense in A Bridges' response to W Blake. It is difficult to imagine that Jesus was not aware of Celtic philosophy, to say the very least.

Celtic peoples left no writings behind about this philosophy but the artefacts which have been unearthed across Europe display cultures of the utmost refinement. Their philosophy, which the druids taught, was transmitted through spoken poetry and through oratory, for the metre of poetry retains a continuity from generation to generation which prose cannot do. (The Jews also knew this.) Their memories were phenomenal. They believed eloquence was more powerful than physical strength – even their enemies admired it. So do the Welsh in their eisteddfods. And 'knowledge', to them, was a spiritual commodity acquired by inspiration; by grace rather than industry. (And so it was incidentally to Martin Luther, the sixteenth-century son of a Saxony miner.)

The druids were also respected arbiters in conflicts both private and public. Like many pre-historic star-gazers they were well acquainted with the movements of heavenly bodies and how these affected the wellbeing of plants and animals here below. They knew about the energies hidden within our Earth, they were Watchers and

Searchers in their total environment, here and in space. To them all things were relative so they naturally drew their moral conclusions from what they found.

Aspiring druids spent up to twenty years in preparation. Collectively they were a fraternity of philosophers, not a sect or a caste or a religion. They were preoccupied, as were all emerging forest dwellers, with the natural order of things. They were intermediaries between humankind and the divine, and their observations guided their conduct and that of their pupils. I understand that both Irish and Welsh mythologies have retained their ease of passing from the natural world to the supernatural and back again without seeming to notice, and their 'land of promise' contains no serious warfare, little that is ugly, no sin or punishment, nothing to cause alarm, few monsters – and their monsters were comical rather than terrifying.

According to the Greek sophist, Dio Chrysostom in about AD100, their influence in the known world was comparable with that of the magi of Persia, the priests of Egypt and the Brahmins of India.

But generalisations about the wide variety of cultural groups labelled 'Celts' which were spread across Europe between these islands and Asia Minor, and spanned centuries either side of the Jesus Event, are limited in usefulness. As they walked out of their wild, prehistoric woodlands into our history books their documented arrival was scant. And generalisations about their druids with a high regard for the oak tree and for magical mistletoe, and with a partiality for head-hunting and human sacrifice are hopelessly inaccurate. The label 'Celt' is itself a lazy generalisation. It would be equally unproductive to dwell upon the barbarism of the Romans who, while portraying the Celts as 'grotesque', could themselves boast the use of crucifixion into the fourth century AD – on one occasion, a thousand in a day.

Human sacrifices were not routine, they occurred at times of conflict when captives provided ample clients. Druids attended them but did not preside, for they were not priests; they were sages and seers concerned with teaching, justice and prophecy. Nevertheless Christians might benefit from studying the primitive and widespread phenomenon of human sacrifice in order to understand their own reference to it better.

If we can thus guess at the nature of the European seedbed where Christianity first germinated two thousand years ago, we might usefully trace some of the roots of Letheringham's present church life: the phenomenon gains an unexpected depth of focus for the outsider, if not also the Christian. Yet the picture is only approximate. It only goes back two or three thousand years. It may contribute to a silhouette of the settlers which our Castle Hedingham dowser said he detected around the church; but who were the people beyond that? A recent find in a South African cave dates the bones of one of our ancestors at two million years ago, so how far back might we usefully go?

Rowan Williams, the present Archbishop of Canterbury, remarked recently that primitive peoples had no word for God; 'wisdom' was 'the mind of God'. The archbishop was looking at two swimming reindeer carved out of a mammoth tusk at the end of the Ice Age about 10,000 years ago when, he said, art and religion were inseparable – unlike today, he said, when religion had become power, and art self-expression. Such peoples were integrated with their environment, he said, and 'at home in the world, part of the flow of life'.

I abandon my thoughts and return to the tower! I exchange a few words with Roger who also has his thoughts. The view from here when the tower was built in 1378 would have been unremitting woodland to the south and west, with perhaps glimpses through the watery trees of the winter river in the north and east. Perhaps the top of the church towers at Easton, Kettleburgh, Hoo and Monewden could be seen through the trees (though I do not know their dates) but Brandeston and Charsfield were entirely out of sight. The church at Hoo is dedicated to St Eustace, a man of very vague origins, said to have been a Roman who, while hunting, was confronted by a deer whose antlers contained a crucifix. So he, with Saints Hubert and Giles, is a patron of hunting, an appropriate dedication for our neck of the woods. The church is actually named after St Andrew as well as St Eustace and I wager that it was the Normans who added Andrew to Hoo's huntsman to make him ecclesiastically respectable. I must find out.

The woodland originally was managed for hunting, primarily, with some banks and ditches to keep the deer in and some to keep them out. Coppicing ash, hornbeam and hazel followed in rotation and was only abandoned seventy years ago. Felling oaks since the Normans was always selective, each tree being bought standing by the purchaser with a particular task in mind – uprights, tie beams, braces, studwork, purlins and rafters – then drawn out of the wood by horses, called sniggers, unless it was very large in which case it was reduced on site using a specially-dug saw pit. The ash were used for a very large number of purposes – like tools and carts because of their supple strength – but anything needed below ground like posts or coffins would require elm if it were to last. The hornbeam was used for axles and cogs because of its hardness, and for firing pottery and brick kilns because it burns so hot. After the felling, self-seeded replacements were protected from deer by a nest of brushwood till they could stand up for themselves. Not a twig was wasted, and the canopy soon closed over the cavity where the felled tree had been.

Thus the people of Letheringham occupied themselves for at least a thousand years up to the First World War.

What is left of Old Park Wood – the five acre strip to the west of the road over the hill from the village to Potsford Brook – reveals a rotational coppicing of hornbeam and ash among the oak, which must have started sometime in the last five or six hundred years where the sixty acres to the west of the road were matched by a similar area to the east of it and north of Lodge Farm – those fields revealingly called the Haugh, the Lawns and

Black Grove. All this woodland would have supplied the timber for the brick industry which developed in the south of the village from the old vicarage up to these trees; it is an area of about thirty-five acres and its fields are called The Brickles to this day. Some of the houses beyond the Forge may have been built as part of the industry, whereas round the Mill there were habitations certainly as old as Domesday and more. The long-abandoned clay pits and sand pits all over the parish would have provided the materials for the bricks.

From this isolated tower however when it was built in about 1350 we could have seen many of the original houses along the Street which predated the ones we see there today, although there is controversy about their age and their original purpose. Roger, for example, thinks that they may have been the original almshouses; Polly says that Mrs Dutton says that the present houses in the Street were built in 1580 and Roger says that the ones up at the church are quite the wrong shape ever to have been almshouses. Yet the dates of the two Nauntons who did all the building are no help in settling the disagreement. All we can assume is that all these cottages and their predecessors have been inhabited by farm workers and brick makers for the past five hundred years at the very least.

The barns and buildings around the Hall and the Mill we could never have seen from up here because of the folds in the land and the watery trees. These and their predecessors go back at least a thousand years.

Up the hill towards the south we can see the top of April Cottage, between Office Farm and Park Farm, which is said to be the oldest house in the village but we do not know if an earlier house existed on that site. It is inhabited today by Terry Carlin and his family. He is in effect the Mayor of Letheringham, though his proper title is Chairman of the Parish Council. He works hard to hold things together and is supportive of the church people, one of whom calls him 'My Leader, he who must be obeyed'.

The supreme economy of the ancient system of forestry was replaced in the twentieth century by our present one whereby a whole woodland is clear-felled and replanted immediately with seedlings usually from abroad; the timber is handled by huge machinery and transported long distances to be processed by more giants. A fraction of the old manpower is needed. The earth is deeply injured, the water tables unbalanced and the wastage huge. The Forestry Commission was started in 1919 to regenerate the country's woodlands which had been badly depleted by the First World War, but it planted far too much alien conifer hoping to get quick returns, and not enough native hardwood which had previously produced the best timber in the world. It also gave grants to landowners to plant trees for timber. In the last few years government policy has changed: I heard with my own ears a Commission executive say to a conference of East Anglian landowners: 'Timber production is no longer on the Commission's shopping list.' The rest of the conference was spent explaining that grants would instead be given to owners of woodland who were kind to ramblers and dormice. Whatever next?

So this is what we are looking at in Letheringham, a total of 25 acres of small scattered woods remaining from about 750 acres when this tower was built. The last big massacre was organised by the Government after the Second World War when they paid landowners 60% grants to remove 'redundant' woodland, hedges and ponds in order to grow more food. It is, in my opinion, a matter of mad imbalance and it is the scandal I wanted to talk about in the mardle. Because, up to a hundred years ago, every parish could boast its own woodland which supplied most of its local necessities, my view of the future is that, as the Big Global Collapse sets in, we shall all need to recover those former self-sufficient practices together with local marketing. But we may not do so in time, I fear, and our grandchildren will marvel at our myopia.

Consequently I look from our ivory tower over the English countryside with some trepidation. The state of agriculture is as fraught as forestry but I know less about it. John Kerr's family farm six thousand acres of land in seventeen local parishes and they are well aware of the dangers. He is active in the local Forum for Sustainable Farming which constantly seeks ways to keep the soil in good heart, reduce erosion, protect water resources and encourage all farmers to be involved with their local communities. He claims, for example, to have over eighty acres in Letheringham where no nitrates have been applied for more than ten years. The Kerrs were founder members of FWAG, the Farming and Wildlife Advisory Group, in Suffolk back in the 1970s, and Suffolk was the second county in the UK to start a group. In 1974 FWAG published a most inspiring report on the farmland in Hoo and Letheringham referring to its history during the last two thousand years and speaking of the land's 'pedigree' being as important to 'the real farmer' as the pedigree of his stock. I myself have certainly seen the organisation's high principles gradually applied since that time in thoroughly practical ways both here and in other parts of England.

John Kerr's parents, William and Mary, came down from Ayrshire in 1938 and started a new life at Abbey Farm with a new dairy herd of their native Ayrshire cattle. They had a good old-fashioned mixed farm until the 1980s when the abolition of the Milk Marketing Board started the terminal decline of dairy farming in East Anglia, finally closing the dairy herd in 2002 when the economics became untenable. John Kerr remembers personally milking cows at Abbey Farm from his earliest years and it was an emotional experience to witness the last dairy cows leaving Letheringham after 64 continuous years of twice a day milking, seven days a week.

Now he and his sons grow salad potatoes for supermarkets and chipping potatoes for fast food outlets such as McDonald's. They are members of a group of farmers producing 18,000 tonnes of green peas for Birds Eye. The more common crops are oilseed rape and wheat, much of which is exported to the continent through

Ipswich docks, and they are grown throughout the parish. Cricket bat willows in the valley of the Deben will end up being exported to Pakistan who make the best bats these days. Edgar Watts of Bungay gave in at the turn of the millennium, and have been succeeded by a former farm student of the Kerr's, Guy Foskett from Eyke, who is making a successful business in the willow trade. Their wheat production has tripled in fifty years; their machine with one driver can do in a day what it once took 15 machines to do in a week.

I am bowled over with admiration for such technological brilliance, who would not be? I just think that, as the Big Global Collapse sets in, we will all be out in those fields with the horses again slaving away to get the goods to Framlingham and Wickham Market. Never mind, they will be nice people to work for, the Kerrs, nice people to chat with as they go about their business, but they'll have to learn to ride a working horse! And it's good to see Fiona Siddall, née Kerr, is breeding Suffolk Punches again at Easton Farm Park.

Chapter 9
CREDO

It is ten weeks since I first came to this church and I have met many of the people involved with it, but still I do not know exactly what they all believe. When I ask them about it they seem to say they believe in a wide range of perspectives but it is hard to find a common factor. The solution, I thought, must surely be found in their creeds, of which there are three in the Book of Common Prayer; and the main one is used in the Mass, or as they say in England, the Communion Service.

The creeds which are recited by the people of Letheringham and by most other congregations in the kingdom go back some seventeen centuries, every single word of them. I have stood among such people from time to time all my life both in England and abroad. We face east and, like a flock of compliant sheep, we rear up on our hind legs and bleat in unison a declaration of our belief in a three-part deity essentially, with sundry bits attached.

Christians are happy to be thought of as sheep by the way because an old man in Ephesus nineteen centuries ago recorded that Jesus, whom he had probably never met, had himself declared that he was The Good Shepherd and his followers his sheep. That analogy goes back twenty-five centuries to Iraq where a homesick exile wrote that he and his compatriots were like lost sheep 'every one to his own way' but that the virtue of their shepherd would redeem them. The shepherd's virtues in turn were sung in a Jewish pop song first recorded thirty centuries ago which, astonishingly, is still sung frequently by popular demand at weddings and funerals today. However, to be sheep-like in any way at all is not a requirement of the Christian creeds.

A good friend of mine, a non-believer, agreed to visit the church with me and discuss the creeds to see what could be found in them, if anything, which was of use to the outsider. As we opened the door a sepulchral voice called out, 'Come in, come in … welcome!' We were looking down at a small man with a bicycle in the porch, plastic bags slung from the handlebars bulging with his belongings. He wore tired leather shoes, pinstriped trousers gathered around his slim waist and a black T-shirt. He had a serious but youthful face, fine-lined with wide open eyes, bright and searching, and vigorous cropped hair. We stepped down into the little porch and we all three started talking, talking about almost everything, and my friend and I sat down on the cold stone sill, wrapped in the man's enthusiasm. His name was Albert. He lived 'for the time being' in a caravan. He said he loved lonely country churches and particularly this one. I asked if he was a Christian and he swallowed and licked his lips and said, well, he wasn't sure. 'I see angels,' he said, 'and I hear them, I hear them when I pray. They're just there,' he said, 'up there,' and he pointed with his hand cupped with respect. 'I prayed not long ago for a woman who was ill. They said I needn't worry. Later I prayed again. They said there's nothing more can be done. You see? I seem to know things before they happen. That's how I am. People think I'm strange. There.'

My friend asked, 'And what do you believe?' and he spoke out at once, 'Ah! There you have it! It's how I live that's what I believe.' Those were his very words. At seventeen he had made 'a big decision' not to live 'like normal people' but to be different, independent, and to 'see things as they really are'.

Suddenly he sat on the floor, upright and with legs straight out before him. He put the tips of his two forefingers and his two thumbs to the floor either side of him at the centre of his gravity and raised his body so that it swung gently from the elbows like a fairground swingboat. After a few moments he lowered himself to the floor again, jumped up and said 'There!' meaning that's what I believe, that says it all. We were dumbfounded. I was reminded of a Roman Catholic bedtime story book long ago in which a clown crept into a church one day and started to juggle before a statue of the Blessed Virgin Mary. When a priest bustled forward to stop him she stepped down from her pedestal smiling and blessed the clown, her hand touching his head. The priest melted back into the shadows.

I cannot remember how this meeting with Albert ended but I do remember shaking hands and resolving to meet again. His hand was strong, the leathery hand of a gardener, for that is how he said he earned his living. When we left the church that day the creeds had not been mentioned.

On the Monday I went to have a cup of tea with Jean Clarke at Letheringham Hall which is the famous moated farmhouse a mile downstream from the church and next to the Mill. The present house is not the original but a relatively modern one. The site has been inhabited since before Domesday by the de Boviles, the Wingfields and the Nauntons, but not for so long by the latter because in 1620 Sir Robert moved up to his newbuild mansion by the church.

The most famous lodger at the Hall had been Henry VIII's red-haired sister, Mary Rose, Duchess of Suffolk and Dowager Queen of France. She had come in 1525 for the hunting. In 1922 Ben Clarke, the Brandeston butcher, bought it with the remaining two hundred acres of farmland; his son Kenneth married Jean and she now continues to farm the land with the help of her son and daughter and a neighbouring farmer. Jean has been a churchgoer for many years and a churchwarden so I asked her what she thought people in the pews believed: 'What do they make of the Nicene Creed, for example?' 'Well,' she said, 'I really don't know about that.' 'But,' I persisted, 'they all say that Creed at the monthly Communion service so I'm just wondering what exactly people mean today when they say, for example, that they believe in 'The Lord Jesus.... being of one substance with the Father by whom all things were made.' She laughed and said, 'Oh, I expect they think different things... and different things at different times. Not many of us are scholars, you know!' So we both laughed and talked of other things.

Nor am I a scholar but I do know of one who lives in Brandeston called Charles Freeman and he has recently visited Letheringham church once or twice. His Suffolk roots run deep. His father's family moved here from Norwich in the 1650s and his mother's, who were Howards, went back even further to Medieval times. He began cycling around Suffolk churches before he learned to drive and he treasured his copy of Henry Munro Cautley's great study of Suffolk churches, poring over its wisdom before each excursion. He enjoys their beauty and delves into their past for he is an historian by trade. At present he is writing a book about medieval relics. The last book he published, called *AD381*, has left me gaping with admiration: he deftly opens up the original documents and writes with such lucidity that it might have happened yesterday.

It appears that in the year 381 the Emperor Theodosius (who was a general, a politician and a townie), fearful of the hoards of pagans (Latin for 'country folk') who were demoralising the already-disintegrating Roman Empire (at that time centred in Constantinople), decreed that if you did not declare your belief in a certain sort of three-part deity as expressed in the Christian creeds you should be charged with heresy. Heresy in the Greek world had long been regarded as an innocent choice-to-think-differently, but now these Romans of the fourth century turned it into a crime.

This is my summary of the book, not the author's. He is concerned to demonstrate that from AD381 'diversity of thought' in the Western world ceased simply because of the imperial edict of Theodosius and his compliant bishops of that time.

Charles Freeman is equally well known for his earlier book *The Closing of the Western Mind* the title of which says it all. I wonder when the Western mind opened up again and recovered its diversity of thought. Was it the Renaissance or the Reformation or the Enlightenment? And is the process continuing in what may come to be called the Scientific Revelation? Perhaps he will write another book.

But this sort of history is too big for me. I am content to look on the church at Letheringham as one of a vast number of such structures in every corner of the world that seem to have survived centuries of conflict, scarred but intact. The phenomenon is curious, for how is it that such small and beautifully simple structures in places like Letheringham can accommodate such complicated formulas which often repel thoughtful well-wishers? The beliefs those formulas aim to express may be simple and beautiful in essence like the buildings themselves, but their meanings seem to be obscured. Yet I have found that simply to be with those people in Letheringham who choose regularly to meet in their lonely sanctuary and recite their complex catechisms in ancient liturgical English strangely inspires me and momentarily pushes aside my search for meaning.

I have the haunting memory of being taken at the age of nine to a concrete church near Sidcup, which was a growing London suburb in Kent, a very different place from Letheringham, partly populated by blitzed refugees from London living in temporary prefabs. It was bomb-damaged and had no light or heat, no organ, but it was full of people and, at the right moment, the priest up at the altar in the east, facing east, boomed out the first four notes of John Merbecke's sixteenth-century Nicene Creed: 'I believe in one God ...'. And after a dramatic pause, as my fond memory would have it, the whole building came alive with corresponding zest: '.... the Father Almighty, Maker of heaven and earth ...' and so on, boldly trundling on to '... the one Lord Jesus Christ ...' with his credentials, and then to '... the Holy Ghost...' and the sundry bits, all swept along by that measured, mystic music and ending with an unexpected flourish: '... and-the-life of-the-world to-come, A-men!' I questioned nothing. God knows what I thought it meant. It did not matter, for I was carried aloft by that crowd of war-weary people in their cold grey building, lifted by their power and poise. Only Orthodox Russia could haunt a child's memory as thrillingly.

But was I duped by the drama? My wife, who was a professional actress when we married, thinks not. In fact she thinks the clergy would benefit if they received some of their training in drama schools.

Since that excitement at Sidcup my own beliefs have swirled about, sometimes pausing at the very gate of heaven and sometimes sinking into the depths of darkness. At all times the creeds and the whole Christian liturgy have been in effect useful inventories, check-lists for the weaker brethren like me, and so I know it is unfair to quiz people on what they believe about the details because, as Jean Clarke said, that varies.

In its earliest days this creed was used in the provinces of the Roman Empire by local magistrates, few of whom called themselves Christians, as a legal reference document in deciding which of the accused before them were guilty of heresy and, consequently who should not be allowed to take over the churches with their estates or be given any other privileges. Even then the language of theology was abstruse for the lesser orders of society. It is no less abstruse for most of us today.

Today, most people, including the church people themselves, find that the trickiest part of the creeds is the Holy Trinity, and when questioned, tend to clamber round the subject in stocking-feet. This is not surprising, for the Trinity is an attempt to define the divine (can it be done?) and to relate Jesus and the rest of us to it. It identifies a three-part deity – the Almighty, Jesus the Christ and the Holy Spirit – but insists that these three are in fact one. To Jews and Moslems it is blasphemy, to atheists rubbish and to many of the early Christians it was plain wrong. To Sir Isaac Newton, three centuries ago in his observatory above the great gate of Trinity College Cambridge, fifty-one miles due west of Letheringham, it made no sense at all – and he was a dedicated churchman. I do not know how many other scholars of the re-opened

Western mind have also dismissed it but as a formula it still has its uses if only to stimulate discussion, because the three-part deity to which it refers describes a relationship between God and humankind. I think it would be better called a two-and-a-halfity in practice, for there are only two so-called 'persons' in the Christian trinity: the Almighty and Jesus. And in operation the relationship between them is a verb, as Albert was saying, not a third substantive as the Emperor Theodosius misleadingly insisted in AD381.

The relationship between Jesus and the Almighty was one of love, a word which can be either verb or noun. For the lovers it is a verb, an activity, whereas for the gossips it is only a noun. Jesus the Jew advocated the lively role of the former, and by the things he did and said he demonstrated the best techniques to his followers. So the third 'person' of the Christian Trinity, the Holy Spirit, can be more usefully described as a half 'person' – if a person at all – and their revered formula *in operation* is better thought of as a two-and-a-halfity.

This is not a game with words. It was written by that giant of Christian thought, Augustine of Hippo in Tunisia, upon whose Rule of Life our Ipswich canons founded their priory at Letheringham. In about AD400 he wrote that the Holy Spirit *was* the mutual love between the 'Heavenly Father' and his 'Beloved Son'. Jesus moreover urged his spellbound followers to be Christlike themselves and independently to have a direct and personal relationship with their 'Father in heaven', as he himself did. So in Letheringham, as in all Christian churches, when they utter a gloria or a doxology (in the name of the Father, the Son and the Holy Ghost...), which is quite often, they are in effect saying 'In the name of divine love...', that universal energy in all creation. The Christian 'Trinity' is their logo for *active love* and, when to outsiders it seems complicated and heavy, that is a great pity because it is in fact the opposite!

The functional view of the Holy Trinity as a two-and-a-halfity is also found in Yoga, as my non-believing friend reminded me. Yoga is a spiritual discipline used by Hindus since at least 500BC, and also by Buddhists. Yogis see us as a trinity of body, mind and spirit; and the secret of its harmony is found through right breathing. So, they believe, the action of the spirit (the breathing) integrates the mind and the body; and in turn, the individual soul is freed to unite with the universal spirit, which union is called Samadhi, bliss. Even if this parallel with the function of the Christian Trinity is no more than a coincidence it is a very happy one, and I wonder why there are not many more practising Christians making use of Yoga in their spiritual gymnasiums. Is this another prejudice handed down by the Romans?

I had read that Betty Mockford was a priest in the Akenfield parishes briefly from 2002 and Letheringham was included within her 'cure' – an ancient term signifying that she had to look after all the 'souls' in her parish including those of the unbelievers. In Craig Taylor's recent book *Return to Akenfield* she was quoted as saying that country people seemed to be more inclined to the concept of a 'Creator God who provides the good earth, the rain and the sunshine.' By contrast she found that in town parishes they seemed to prefer 'a much more Jesus-based faith'.

This is an interesting observation. If it is accurate, the phenomenon must surely be caused by country people being surrounded by countryside and town dwellers by people: the former are closer to the primitive concepts of their religion while the latter have long since preoccupied themselves with the sociological demands of living close together. This is a little simplistic, I expect, but it's fun.

I wonder in what way Betty Mockford found that country people appear to be more inclined to a 'Creator God' than town people. Might it be their choice of prayer book? Letheringham, which uses Archbishop Cranmer's 1662 Book of Common Prayer, is among the parishes which did not change to the new Common Worship when it came out in 2000. Cranmer was a Nottinghamshire lad and a poetic, diffident scholar of Jesus College, Cambridge, and he was the progeny of a rural population, whereas the compilers of the new book were, like many of us today, of urbanised, industrialised and egalitarian stock. Both teams used much the same material which dates from the first five centuries but Cranmer was translating whereas the new book is an adaptation. Cranmer's language was not the colloquial register of his time but liturgical, repetitive to aid memory, poetic and very respectful of the Almighty. The new adaptation is less deferential, closer to the plain English of the man in the street and more instructional, less devotional. A young Oxford priest, a good friend, told me that 'Almighty' is not a very 'fashionable' word these days, and I think many of the new modifications may have been governed by that sort of criterion. The new Communion Service uses the title half as often as old Cranmer does.

The focus of Cranmer's plain Morning and Evening Prayers is very similar to that in his Holy Communion. One gets the feeling his services were intended, at least on paper, to be an amorous tryst between a bunch of happy admirers and their Maker. They know, as every lover knows, that what they are doing is far-fetched, romantic and beyond the normal bounds of reason; their voices are hushed, their language folded with hidden meaning, they bow, they go down on their knees, they clasp their hands, then rise up and sing their madrigals and their eulogies. Such behaviour would disturb the peace at a bus stop; luckily there are none in Letheringham so instead they gather discreetly in the pretty seclusion of their country church.

The printed words alone, however, are not the only worry of people in their churches. The way the words are delivered is of equal concern to them. As my wife says, a good actor can give wings to a lousy script and a bad one can slaughter a masterpiece. Lucky Letheringham with its relays of visiting retired clergy and its 1662 Prayer Book often gets the best on both counts.

In the big outside world, by which I mean Europe and

The West generally, the most prevalent religion at the moment, particularly among people who are young at heart, is Ecology – the intercourse of the individual with the 'environment'. It has its formulas for belief and for behaviour, its political correctnesses and esoteric language, its temples, priesthood, university courses and even its hagiography. It also has its hypocrites. But its active members look upon their 'environment' with admiration, even with awe, and are often deeply committed to an intimate relationship with it, protecting it, acting in harmony with it, husbanding it, healing it, making significant sacrifices in their own lives for its sake. On the matter of its origin however their views are usually muted. Is this out of respect? Or scientific modesty? Or maybe it is for fear of falling into the traps of organised religion: sentimental titles like Father are not used and, as for Creator, it is often met with derision thanks to the utterances of those wacky fundamentalist Christians who cannot cope with Darwin. Indirectly, Ecology is a robust form of Christianity where the concept of the divine is focussed closer to home than that of the ancient star-gazers with their long-range vision found in documents like the Old Testament part of the Bible. Ecologists revere the marvellous beauty, the balances and the intricacy of our planet cradled in her cosmos while Christians, many of whom are similarly inclined, choose to persevere with identifying and worshipping its source as well. Worship is a good old-fashioned Anglo-Saxon word meaning 'to respect the worth of', and you don't have to be religious to do it.

The churchgoers of Letheringham are among those people who are ecologically aware and one of them has commissioned, with the Archdeacon's approval, the local artist Tessa Newcomb, to paint a triptych for the north wall illustrating all the life of the surrounding countryside. Words from Psalm 24 will be painted into it: 'The earth is the Lord's and the fullness thereof; the world and they that dwell therein.' Tessa says it is an unusual experience for her to be leaving her work behind with the people she is depicting, not stealing it away. It is, she says, 'a celebration of the parish and the presence of the people in the parish' and she feels her gift is like a mirror for them. The earth for her is indeed 'the Lord's' although she prefers to speak of 'the life force' and things like 'the burgeoning shoots of spring' rather than the conventional three-lettered word which Christians tend to use so freely.

It is said that an artist, a creator, cannot be separated from the creatures of his or her passion, and the Christians think this also applies to 'The Maker of heaven and earth' and, in reciprocating what they see as his love for them, they are bound also to love their fellow creatures. As St Bernard said in Clairvaux half a century before Letheringham's present priory church was built: 'Love me, love my dog'. Surely he was blithely re-stating that gem of Jewish wisdom which the Christians had commandeered a thousand years before. Jesus the Jew had naturally quoted it and it reached the English language via the Greek with vibrant clarity: Love and serve God above all, and love your neighbour as yourself.

But who is my neighbour? Early one bright blue and golden Suffolk morning I telephoned a friend in Greece called Irene who translates Greek books into English and she assured me that the Greek root of the word 'neighbour' is nearness of people or surroundings brought about by approaching them or drawing them to yourself; a wide meaning. So 'environment' is a close cousin and 'ecology' derives from the Greek for a house, a household, the domestic scene, implying families and social intercourse. I checked this with a Baptist minister in Framlingham who knows Hebrew, a jolly man of 84, and he said much the same: 'neighbour' to the Hebrew was a general term, he said, and it could mean friend, associate, lover, colleague, fellow-citizen or somebody who lived nearby.

The Letheringham people I have met so far all appear to believe in this second part of the Jewish Law which the Christians commandeered: they are all very neighbourly. It is not an easy age to be neighbourly because we are all so domestically insulated these days but, as things get harder, I think we will be brought closer to each other for company and protection, as in times past.

The people who go to church – and some who do not – also set out to believe in the first part of the Jewish Law which is to revere a supreme authority in the universe above and beyond all their earthly doings, yet inherently related to their doings. This is the churchgoers' common denominator and it is very scientific. However one chooses to define or name that supreme authority, its character and esteem among humans is the oldest science in the world. The science has consisted, for as far back as we can tell, in a keen observation of and respect for what they have usually regarded as the origin of all existence, both seen and unseen. And they have evolved their earthly moralities from that study. They have looked long at the sun and the moon, the planets and the stars beyond and have concluded that what they find here on earth is variously connected. This faith is reflected in the new triptych in the church at Letheringham.

As I see it, the arguments about science as against theology are very silly. The origin of the universe and the dawn of life on this particular planet are not subjects peculiar to modern science. Today's cosmogonists and protozoologists did not invent them. They were always of compelling interest to our distant forbears who demonstrated their fascination and their reverence – not mere respect – for the movements of the heavenly bodies, the physical laws of planet Earth and all forms of life herein. So in the old universities theology was not referred to as the queen of the sciences carelessly. And the moralities of our distant forbears took shape from the laws of nature as they saw them. Celestial geometry was sacred, as also became the geometry of their buildings from the earliest times; the moral term 'righteousness' for example was to them originally an architectural term, and 'to sin' was to miss the target when aiming to harmonise with the laws of nature. I think this perspective is relevant to what goes on inside churches like Letheringham, where services retain the ghosts of primordial liturgies.

Judaism, among those distant cultures, distilled all such values over the centuries and acclaimed their pre-eminence and beauty in its philosophy and poetry. Within the resulting pottage, quite suddenly, Christianity crystallised and, in spite of the distortions of fourth-century Romanisation, it has become the essence of what the church people of Letheringham enjoy today. They find it hard to describe this in a neat reply about belief because it is so large. Everyone finds it hard. Their belief, in keeping with the other Christians, is a comprehensive and a truly materialistic faith in *all that is*, visible and invisible, and their faith is inseparable from their deep reverence for its origin: which they aim to worship.

There is nothing zany about worship. It may be an old-fashioned Anglo-Saxon word but its meaning is as much worldly as it is spiritual and in practice it is an animal process as wholesome as breathing and feeding. Because Christian worship is particularly woven with the dynamics of love, one could be forgiven for imagining that its participants should turn out to be good and amiable citizens; and for being disappointed when sometimes they don't. There was a rumour in the very early church that their secret meetings (secret for fear of Roman persecution) were called 'love-feasts' (in Greek) because they were suspected of being orgies and not, as they claimed, Eucharists (thanksgivings) for the abundant love of the Creator as recommended by Jesus.

That ancient view of things is marvellously summed up in Alexander Pope's *Essay on Man* which appeared just after the death of Newton. Here are three brief extracts:

All are but parts of one stupendous whole,
Whose body Nature is, and God the soul;
That, changed through all, and yet in all the same;
Great in the earth, as in the ethereal frame;
Warms in the sun, refreshes in the breeze,
Glows in the stars, and blossoms in the trees;
Lives through all life, extends through all extent;
Spreads undivided, operates unspent!
Breathes in our souls, informs our mortal part,
As full, as perfect in a hair as heart;
As full, as perfect in vile man that mourns,
As the rapt seraph that adores and burns:
To him no high, no low, no great, no small;
He fills, he bounds, connects and equals all …

and

See, through this air, this ocean, and this earth,
All matter quick and bursting into birth.
Above, how high, progressive life may go!
Around, how wide, how deep extend below!
Vast chain of being! which from God began,
Natures ethereal, human, angel, man,
Beast, bird, fish, insect, what no eye can see,

No glass can reach; from infinite to thee,
From thee to nothing …

and

From Nature's chain whatever link you strike,
Tenth or tenth thousandth, breaks the chain alike.

Pope was a Londoner, crippled since the age of twelve by 'too much reading' some said, but he became a passionate gardener and that must surely have contributed to his enlightened ecological outlook.

From the very beginning, however, churches have made their own type of poetry in the form of rhymes and songs, and used them as an instrument of worship, so I went again to the church at Letheringham to see how their hymnal describes the source of all that is, visible and invisible. I hoped it would disclose more of what the people believed. This research rewarded me with a colourful sequence of thought.

The uninhibited hymn-singers, echoing the thoughts of those who wrote the hymns, describe the object of their devotions as 'He … whose robe is light, whose canopy space' and in whose sight 'a thousand ages … are like an evening gone'. They visualise a being of human form and of male gender. They have described it like that from the earliest times. (And the earth they saw as female.) But 'He', they were sure, is powerful and 'strong to save, whose arm doth bind the restless wave'; and he is everlasting, 'who changest not'; he has been their 'help in ages past' and will be their 'hope for years to come'. They are confident that he will, in some as-yet-unspecified way, become their 'eternal home'. So they appear to believe that he is not confined to the realms of time and space and is more easily perceived in a realm of light which is 'immortal' and 'invisible' and 'inaccessible, hid from our eyes', and they sing 'O help us to see, 'tis only the splendour of light hideth thee'.

Such is the might and stature of this entity that they sometimes feel the need for agents to 'assist' their 'song', otherwise, they find, 'the theme too high doth seem for mortal tongue'. These agents are the 'bright... angels... who wait at God's right hand or... fly, at their Lord's command... through the realms of light'. 'Angels help us to adore him' they explain because angels can 'behold him face to face', whereas they, being mere mortals, are only lowly 'dwellers in time and space' who, like the 'sun and moon', need to 'bow down before him', such is his dazzling glory.

The vocabulary of these hymn singers is particularly exciting because it reveals them juggling with the same vast components of Einstein's famous equation – energy, matter, time, space and light – and implying, as he did, that these components are all interdependent and each constantly adjusting to the changes in the others; it is only energy that 'operates unspent', as Pope had it, or as the writer of the hymn 'Abide with Me' addressed it a hundred years later, 'thou who changest not'; and Einstein also said that it was indestructible even though it was constantly transforming. While I was thinking about all this recently I happened to hear the Archbishop of Canterbury in an Ascension Day sermon speaking about that 'depth of energies out of which all things come' and explaining that, at the end, Jesus became 'at one with that universal energy'.

The language of the hymn writers is no more arcane than that of today's cosmologists because, from Galileo to Newton to Einstein to our own space age people, the scientists have always been speaking of things beyond every-day language and on the edge of the unknown. But I did hear the enthralling Professor Brian Cox of Manchester bringing the subject down closer to our pedestrian level in a lecture: 'After the Big Bang darkness was banished ...' he said. 'There was a universal stretching ... Our galaxy is a symphony of light ... We can see how light breathes life into us ... Our own existence depended upon the death of a star somewhere out there ... The most beautiful thing about Einstein's theory of the universe is that it is incomplete, it is on the edge of the unknown ...' (I understand Einstein himself acknowledged this.)

It seems to me that the basic material of the hymn singers is much the same as that of the diligent scientist. They are all fascinated by the same mysteries – the origins of the universe, the nature of life on this planet and the phenomenon of human consciousness – and the two camps are only separated by the way they proceed. The hymn singer is a dramatist who sees a creator, classifies him as a male and speaks affectionately of him in human terms, whereas the atheistic scientist – they are not always atheists – is a hunter equipped with keen-edged reason and a noble determination to define the truth. This is a very testing task and I wonder if the scientists might benefit from time to time if they were to join the hymn singers for a little light relief. Irritation with their methods would not last for ever and they might find themselves happily transported into their land of make-believe for a while.

The lyrical hymn-singers look not only to the heavens. They also look about themselves at 'Dear mother earth who, day by day, unfoldest blessings on our way'. When they see 'the earth with her wonders untold', they ask 'what tongue can recite' her cornucopia of 'bountiful care?' They conclude that the Maker of it all is 'most wonderful... in all his works... most sure in all his ways' and that they should 'let all mortal flesh keep silence and... stand ... with awe, and welcome' him; and they should 'let sense be dumb, let flesh retire' for they will hear him 'speak through earthquake, wind and fire' in his 'still, small voice of calm'.

So, about identifying and communicating with this almighty entity, the hymn-singers are very specific. They concede that he does indeed 'move in a mysterious way... to perform... his wonders' but, 'behind a frowning providence', they assert, 'he hides a smiling face'. They also observe that 'A man that looks on glass, on it may stay his eye; or, if he pleaseth, through it pass, and then the heavens espy'.

What they see through the glass is a creator, fatherlike and majestic, and they respond with: 'Praise to the Lord, the Almighty, the King of Creation!' their shouts borne aloft no doubt by angels with trumpets. He is their Maker and they are among 'all creatures of' their 'God and King' ranging from 'tall trees ... purple-headed mountains ...' and 'each little bird that sings' to 'thou burning sun with golden beam ... silver moon ... clouds ... flowing water'. 'My God!' they exclaim, 'How wonderful thou art, thy majesty how bright!'

However, when things go badly or monsters like 'earthquake, wind and fire' harm them, their song becomes timorous: 'I do not ask to see the distant scene' they reflect, 'One step enough for me', and they pray 'Lead, kindly light, amid the encircling gloom... the night is dark and I am far from home...' their soft melody fading as choirs of Welsh miners thunder Cwm Rhondda from the west: 'Guide me, O thou great Jehovah, pilgrim through this barren land; I am weak but thou art mighty – hold me in thy powerful hand'.

So they see life as a journey: 'O for a closer walk with God' they dream, but it is a journey with a purpose: 'Awake, my soul,' they call, 'and, with the sun, thy daily stage of duty run. Shake off dull sloth and joyful rise ...' and they bid all those whose 'first avowed intent' is 'to be a pilgrim' to remain 'constant ... come wind, come weather'. They pray 'Teach me, my God and King, in all things thee to see; and what I do in any thing, to do it as for thee'. And, to their own souls they sing: 'bear thou thy part ... and ... sing thou the songs of love; let all thy days till life shall end be filled with praise'.

They sing a lot about the time when 'life shall end'. They don't believe death is the end; for them it is none other than 'the gate of life immortal'! At this point, I imagine, an outsider would clear his throat, for comprehension has been wearing a bit thin. 'How come?' I hear him ask politely. 'How is death a gate to more life?' They don't reply. Instead they sing more hymns about love and light, about transformations and how the ends are also beginnings. The Polite Outsider withdraws, smiling inwardly, and mutters, 'You sound just like the astronomers, and I'm none the wiser!'

As for references to Jesus in the hymns, they are plentiful as the flowers in spring. The singers seem to see in that distant Galilean the same attributes which they observed in the Almighty. Jesus is for them the embodiment of the Creator himself and they sing : 'Never was love, dear King ... like thine!' and 'This is my friend, in whose praise I could gladly spend all my days', and they ask, 'Who am I, that, for my sake, my Lord should take frail flesh and die?'

The comprehension of the more prosaic onlookers may flag at this point but, for the singers, it is through the words and works of that marvellous man 'beside the Syrian sea' that their heavenly Maker becomes personal to each of them. Their view is definitely different from that of the ordinary man in the street. They positively regard life and sustenance as gifts from above, rather than commodities to be demanded from 'society' as their 'human rights'. Consequently, for them, 'the brotherhood of man' is a reality by virtue of the Almighty's fatherhood rather than from the dull imposition of some egalitarian regime.

Some literati from Dr Samuel Johnson onwards have criticised the limitations of hymnody, one rudely describing it as 'the Bible chopped up and crucified' with its 'stiff quatrains shovelled out four-square'! Hymns may be an acquired taste but they serve well to reveal to me a general flow of thought and belief. One or two come from the earliest times. Others are the poetry of intervening centuries up to that of George Herbert and John Bunyan, but most were written from the eighteenth century onwards as hymns to be sung in churches. Some are dreary, some are barmy and utterly unsingable, but I find there are many which are plain beautiful.

My research was complete. I went outside and sat for a while on the new bench which Rebecca Rice's parents had given. It is peaceful here. Now I am the outsider and the little church appears to be bigger than usual, the flintwork brighter, the red bricks redder. My vision is changing in the open air. I muse.

Perhaps it was presumptuous of me to attempt a summary of what people believe in this building. Perhaps Jean Clarke was right: 'Different things at different times' may be as close as we can hope to get. Or, if Albert is right, I might have done better to scrutinise the churchmongers' private lives. But, as they say, only God can do that.

I met Albert again long after all this. He was cycling

fast to Benhall early in the morning with a thermos in a small canvas bag over his shoulder. I asked if I could quote what he had said about belief. He looked puzzled.

'What did I say?'

'You said, 'It's how I live that's what I believe."

'Did I say that?'

'Yes, you did!'

'Really?'

'Yes, you did, Albert, and it's exactly what Jesus used to say.'

His blue eyes opened wide as wide can be and he uttered, 'Did he? … Did he really? … Well!' and, smiling to himself, he prepared to hurry away.

'Yes, yes!' I called as he pedalled off, 'and can I put it in my book?'

'Oh yes!' he shouted and disappeared into the trees round Bigsby's Corner.

Chapter 10
ROOKS

My first thought on Friday 23rd March was how little time was left. I dressed nervously. Outside, a fine day, rather chilly, but the chickens were already busy in the orchard after light night rain and I filled my lungs with the keen air. The postman delivered the slides for the mardle, so I need not have worried, and they were beautiful, exactly as I had planned. I glanced through my notes: now I could look safely down on Monday's ordeal and try to enjoy the prospect.

I drank some tea with Josephine, my wife, and set out alone for Letheringham. At the church I dwelt a pause: there she stood, my now-familiar friend, definitely feminine, beaming approval: St Mary of Letheringham, whose virtues I was planning to commend in Monday's mardling.

From the gatehouse I walked up to Robert Curtis's remaining trees following the route the first pilgrims from Ipswich had used, along the cleavage between the two parishes of Letheringham and Hoo. I crossed a little bridge and slipped into the wood where I stood for a time absorbing the mood. A magpie flew out guiltily and a muntjac sauntered off insolently along a bank. The ground was littered with dry sticks and signs of other creatures. The trees were tall and bare. A slight breath of air rattled their top branches, mainly ash and hornbeam sprung rudely from stools abandoned some seventy years before. It was a cold wood and I sighed deeply and felt pains in my chest which must have resulted, I thought, from too much writing at home.

I moved in as quietly as possible and found a mound from which I could look through the leafless underwood down to my friend in the distance. The warming morning sun smiled on her and I felt very happy looking out from this cold place. There was a wide stretch of grassland along this northern edge where I think horses were exercised and as I looked across it to the church below a man walked in the grass slowly from my left to my right. I stood still, not wanting to be seen. I was in no mind for conversation. He was a smallish man, not so young or upright, with a protruding jaw and receding brow, his gaze fixed on the lemony sun rising through the naked trees. He may have been wearing a brownish jerkin and blue jeans, or bluish something. I could hear no sound at all. When he had gone I turned into the centre of the wood and thought no more of it. I was trying to feel the age of that place and pick up some memory of the wild context from which the Priory had emerged.

The pains in my chest persisted and I looked up, heaving a sigh and seeking comfort from the blue sky beyond the branches but, stepping back, I lost my balance and fell into a slight hollow behind me. It was lined with fine brushwood and, finding it comfortable, I fell to laughing and looking upwards with great ease and increasing interest. I felt no urge to get up but lay like a child in a crib marvelling at the tallness of the trees, the tininess of the topmost twigs, the blueness of the sky beyond, the awesome height of heaven.

I could see rooks circling high above the trees and heard distantly the occasional quack, a sharp note which I had always taken to be the order of the duty lance-corporal responsible for guiding them down. They came lower and I watched with a fascination I had had since my youth as they wove their patterns. Then I realised I was becoming dizzy: was I seeing the birds in relation to the trees or vice versa? My head was swimming, they were descending; next they were landing, some quite low down all around, all chattering and chortling; others perched in the higher branches yet all with strangely uncharacteristic fearlessness.

Next I distinctly heard one of them croak, 'What's he up to?' And another higher, older one shouted down, 'Watch out he hasn't got a gun,' to which a lower one replied, 'No, he's not armed,' and a third, much younger one, cackled, 'He's unarmed and he's legless,' whereupon most of them flew up again consumed with laughter and then, one by one, resettled closer to have a better view.

The higher, older one announced, 'He's lost something,' and the chorus resumed below with, 'What's he lost?' and 'He can't remember', and 'He will when he finds it.'

A rather scruffy bird out on a limb mused, 'Those poor

folk down there, no time for thought,' and several others muttered agreement, and one remarked, 'Too much writing, too much reading,' to which a bad-tempered, older one who was looking the other way turned her head and grunted, 'Information inflammation', and they all agreed, one of them adding rather donnishly, 'Too much knowledge, heads expanding, bodies weakening', and a colleague on the same branch added, 'Scarce able to walk, some of them', to which a youngster lower down squawked, 'Let alone fly!' at which their laughter exploded and they launched into the air again unable to contain themselves. This time, some of them flew off in a south-easterly direction as, I assumed, they had duties or pleasures elsewhere. But the rest resettled still closer. I wanted to speak but no words came.

There was a new atmosphere. They seemed to be talking quietly among themselves, some preening themselves rather nervously I thought, some shifting to better branches, the smaller ones closer to the larger ones. It was clear to me their prologue was over. I was impressed by their performance and wanted to ask them to continue. I felt I had something to learn from them. But no words came.

The higher, older bird who was extremely black responded to my thoughts by suddenly proclaiming in a very long sentence for a rook: 'You lot have forsaken your high places, you have abandoned your regular gatherings and you've forgotten how to worship.' I wanted to object but he responded even before I had constructed a sentence: 'Oh, I know, I know, you make a stab at it in your little church down there but you are only fifteen per cent of the population of Letheringham and ...' He was interrupted by a studious, bespectacled bird with, 'Forgive me, Lord Cawking, but that's a pretty high rating: most parishes feel pleased if they reach five percent.' He ignored her.

'Worship is making love,' he went on. 'You do it with your body and your ingenuity, not your brain; as servants, not masters.' Then the lower chorus began to chip in again with rhythmic beak-snapping and groovy undertones.

'Your churches,' he went on, 'were built like the temples of Sûmer and they in turn were like the sacred groves your distant forebears used in these parts: the way you process up your aisles is not an architectural accident, it's ...' But the bespectacled bird interrupted again: 'Oh come, come, my Lord. That's too near the talon for this sanitised lot.' More laughter and applause. As it subsided he swooped down and perched right next to me, a little above my head. I had never seen a living rook so close before and marvelled at his vibrant beauty. There cannot be a blacker black in all the earth, nor a more intriguing beak, a brighter or more knowing eye, a more elegantly hosed leg, a more engaging swagger. He said in a corvine sotto voce, 'And tell your grandsons to read about Plato and his Cave. It may help a bit.'

With that he took off, as they all did together, and great was the commotion thereof what with the beating wings and the coarse and joyous shouting. They went quickly up, out of the wood. A single breast feather floated down and settled silent upon my jacket.

I asked my wife to fetch a glass of warm, salty water for a toothache and she flew off. When she returned she was not my wife but the bluish old man who had been walking through the grass. He was very, very, very old and looked deeply into me. I thought I knew him. With soft leathery hands he stroked my cheek and put the glass to my lips. He lay with me for a while and I received much consolation.

When I awoke, straightway I started back down the hill, blissfully refreshed and basking in a blanket of painlessness, indulging my memory with these extraordinary dreams, determined not to let the nimblest detail escape. I moved with ease, as if on air, clambering over the churchyard wall like an eleven-year-old and pausing to take in the scene. What a scene, by Jove! What a place of cool, celestial sanity!

The car climbed up from the village and over the hill by Old Park Wood. As I passed the field on the left, which is called the Haugh, I saw the rooks again. They were feeding on the far side between the two oaks and some of them on the nether side of the ditch rose up, circled a little and settled again to their afternoon meal.

Chapter 11
MONEY

Saturday 24th March, a grey day. I woke worrying about the things I was planning to say on Monday about the money. There was such a lot to say and I had no illustrations. Should I shorten it? Should I print a summary? Should I omit it altogether?

While I made tea I remembered it was Gabriel's birthday. Aged four, he was the youngest of the three grandsons. I felt ashamed that I had not opened my eyes to that memory instead of the money. It was too early to ring him so I lit a fire and thought about him. Like all children, he is a miracle. His parents had secretly decided some time before his birth to call him Gabriel so when we discovered some time later that he had turned up on the ancient feastday of the Archangel Gabriel, that radiant herald of divine love, we were all flabbergasted. Of the three archangels in Christian mythology, Gabriel has the clearest definition even though he is only mentioned four times in the Bible. And he goes back a very long way before Bible times to at least the third millennium BC, probably much further, when he was regarded in Lebanon as the leader of no less than seven archangels. The other two Christian archangels – Michael who has often been confused down the ages with George and his dragon, and

Raphael the patron saint of healing – are more blurred, but Gabriel's role is cool and sensational. And it is his feast day today because tomorrow is Lady Day.

Wallowing in these memories of four years ago, I poured myself another cup of tea and the day was no longer grey. Letheringham's budget is very small but it is a useful miniature of the problems that the other 460-odd parishes in the diocese have to cope with. Letheringham is so small that one can almost sympathise with an inclination among chairborne administrators to abolish it, or at the least amalgamate it somehow. The vicarage of the days of *Akenfield* was sold long ago, and it has not been able to afford its own priest for as long as most people can remember. It is now scheduled to share one with seven other parishes, for there simply are not enough priests to go round. So the village has no priest of its own, no school, no shop, no pub and no policeman. But it does have a church.

The parish covers an area of about 1200 acres, not the smallest but the diocesan average is about 2,000 acres. The parish's population is said to be 65 souls; the diocesan average is 1300 souls. There are, incidentally, some much larger ones: St Mary's Woodbridge has about 6,000 as do parishes in Felixstowe, Hadleigh, Sudbury and Ipswich. But Ipswich is exceptional: St Mary at Stoke has 13,000 while St Francis has 18,000 and these large parishes are of course administered by a team of clerics.

It is easy to see therefore that such large populations must be balanced by many much smaller ones to explain the average of 1300. In Letheringham's group, the eight populations total about 1600: Hoo 85, Monewden 100, Dallinghoo 150, Cretingham 180, Ashfield cum Thorpe 180, Charsfield with Debach (they sold the church at Debach) 425 and Earl Soham (where the new priest in charge will live) 415.

These eight parishes form what they call a benefice, of which there are five in the so-called Loes Deanery, with the Rural Dean residing in the largest parish of St Michael's, Framlingham. It has a population of about 2500 and a very fine church. The Priest in Charge is a lively, musical man with an air of enjoyment about him. As Rural Dean he has to care for the pastoral needs of the clergy in the twenty parishes of his deanery. When I asked him for the meaning of life he was very busy: 'Probably 42', he said, and hurried away. Later that day, Michael Knight, a bright-eyed youth of Ashfield-cum-Thorpe who was presiding at the Co-op checkout in the town, assured me that it certainly was 42 and he was surprised that I was not more familiar with hitchhikers and galaxies. I was abashed for Barney had already told me, 'It's time you read that book, Grandpa.' Michael had a Norwich degree in mathematics. Does that give him more credibility or less than a clergyman in this matter?

The Loes Deanery is one of six in the northeast of Suffolk and together they form an archdeaconry. Archdeacons in this county have usually been three in number although I believe there is one absent at the moment. Ours is called the Archdeacon of Suffolk, and the other two are of Ipswich and Sudbury. An archdeacon is a very important senior priest whose job is to know about every detail of the fabric of his churches and about the life of all his parishes and their clergy. No structural alteration to the churches and churchyards may be undertaken without his express permission; but above him is the Chancellor of the Diocese whose word on graver matters is final – the selling of a church for example. An archdeacon is at the same time in constant touch with his bishop, giving advice and assisting in appointments and many other matters. It is a big job. I have met a few archdeacons over the years and they always seem to be unexpectedly jovial people. When I was a boy, one of them still wore black gaiters with buttons all the way up the sides, a relic of the days when they had to spend much of their time on horseback. All that may soon return. We shall see!

In the great diocesan pool, therefore, Letheringham is a very small fish yet, as a parish – a three-sided piece of land lying between a river, a brook and similar features along which people and animals used to find their way – it is a very significant territory and much older than the diocese, well over a thousand years older. I believe Christians of a sort in Britain must have lived here from the first century AD. Bishops of a sort in Britain go back to about the third century, but their dioceses did not begin to emerge from the old Saxon kingdoms until about the seventh century.

Eorpwald the king of East Anglia became a Christian in about AD600 and, soon after, St Felix the Burgundian, was made the first Bishop of Dunwich and talk of North-folk and South-folk began, but it was not until about 1100 that Bert the Lozenge moved his headquarters from first Elmham, then Thetford, to Norwich and built the cathedral dedicating it to 'The Holy and Undivided Trinity' to be administered by a Benedictine monastery. As for the South-folk, they only split off to form a separate diocese at the outbreak of the First World War: 'The Diocese of St Edmundsbury and Ipswich,' such an awkward title, covers Suffolk but excludes Lowestoft. I know not why.

So although the diocese which covers most of Suffolk started in Dunwich strictly speaking some 1400 years ago, it only really came into its own about 100 years ago and is only just completing the building of its supremely elegant lantern tower on the cathedral at Bury St Edmunds. Its choice of title – the Diocese of St Edmundsbury and Ipswich –seems to be unfortunate for it stresses the historic divisions between the cultural west and the commercial east of the land. Perhaps as the Great Global Collapse hits us the Bishop will be constrained to move his offices to Stowmarket which is the geographically central town of Suffolk; and that would certainly reduce the administrative cost of the diocese, as well as demonstrating its unity. A battery of portacabins in the station yard would be much more accessible and economical than the present plush apartments in Ipswich.

The diocesan office in Ipswich has a great deal of work to do. It collects £6.4 million from the parishes in the year

(2008/9). This collection is called 'The Parish Share'. Three quarters of this sum goes to the clergy, their training, payment, maintenance and pensions. Only one quarter goes to pay for its own work which is now a very large concern. I have not been able to discover how efficiently the millions are spent, and if I had, probably another book would be needed.

The Diocesan Secretary is the top man in the diocesan office and with him are accountants, lawyers, registrars, architects, surveyors, librarians, communicators and sundry clerks. They are in touch with a large number of chaplains and specialists out in the parishes who advise on or supervise such matters as vocations, the training of clergy, elders and readers, in-service courses, retired clergy and widows; then there is missionary work, contacts with other denominations and religions, pastoral care, youth work, church schools, agriculture, urban matters, tourism, emergencies, hospitals and healing. The full time office staff have to be paid properly but the advisers tend only to be given transport and other small expenses. Nevertheless the administration of the diocese is a very considerable expense.

As for the parish of Letheringham, the sixty-five people who live there need to find about £10,000 a year to keep their church building in healthy working order. Their church it is because it legally belongs to them, being resident within the boundaries of its parish and regardless of their individual beliefs. About sixteen of them know this and have signed on as Church Electoral Rollers. They make contributions in finance and half of them make very big contributions in time and energy as well as in finance: they are the eight members of the PCC (Parochial Church Council, as compared with the civil Parish Council). The PCC in Letheringham is a sort of ginger group. These are the details (in the year 2008/9) of what they have to find annually, to the nearest £250:

PAYMENTS

to the cost of CLERGY, paid to the diocese who in turn will supply them with one eighth of a priest, when he or she has been appointed: 2750

to the cost of DIOCESAN ADMINISTRATION in the Ipswich offices: 1000

to all their own domestic RUNNING COSTS from things like insurance and electricity to books, candles, polish and flowers (many of which they themselves supply free):
1750

to the cost of REPAIRING THE FABRIC of the church after the diocesan architect assessed and made his estimates: 2500

to the cost of IMPROVEMENTS HOPED FOR, such as new churchyard lighting and a toilet: 2000

(These last two items have been averaged over five years)

So these payments must be found each year: £10,000

RECEIPTS

At present they only manage to raise about £7000 a year and the following details are also to the nearest £250:

from PLANNED GIVING AND MONEY-RAISING EVENTS such as mardles organised by the ginger group:

6000

from COLLECTIONS AT SERVICES; some sent away to charities: 1000

from THE WALL SAFE – average of 90 visitors a year give very little: 0

So at present (2008/9) they receive this amount each year:

£7000

Thus the shortfall is about £3,000 a year at the moment. It could scarcely be bridged by spending less: they run the place on a shoe-string already and even do some of the repairs themselves. Their biggest expense is the Parish Share. I see they are charged at the rate of £55 a head of population, yet the average in the eight churches of this benefice is only £25 a head, and in the whole diocese only

£11 a head. This seems oddly unfair. If instead Letheringham were charged at the benefice rate their shortfall would be halved, and at the diocesan rate it would be wiped out. Does someone somewhere wish to close Letheringham down, I wonder?

The Parochial Church Council in Letheringham is a very laid-back group of eight or ten people who do absolutely everything themselves. They hunt round for priests to come during the interregnum, they clean and polish the church, arrange flowers, play the organ, assemble small choirs, groom the churchyard and do the odd repair. They also raise money by mardling, having parties by the river, selling stuff and, once, they had a car boot sale. They seem to pay many of the costs themselves: cups of tea and buns, hire of halls, transport, time and so on. Their ages range from 30 to 80 years. Some of them are seasoned villagers but others have only been there for five or ten years. They are all very different in character and background but together they are a delightful team, very welcoming and undemanding people to be with, not rabid money raisers at all. They are a veritable ginger group and you feel all the better for being with them.

Their efforts to raise money however are enormous and also discreet: the church is not hung about with arresting notices about costs and appeals. Yet their bank balance is precariously low and their assets almost nil. Figures like this can terrify people out of their wits, but if the Letheringham group are alarmed they do not parade it. If you ask them how they will find the money, they smile and mutter something about feeling sure it will turn up one way or another. Meanwhile they continue to organise services and things with patent enjoyment and at almost zero cost. It is a phenomenon which is more or less repeated by some 16,000 Parochial Church Councils throughout the land, though I don't know how many of them can match the style of Letheringham's.

The Church in England has never before found it so hard to raise the money to keep things going. This is only partly due to the reduction in churchgoing, I suspect, and more fundamentally because it has finally said goodbye to the ancient system of tithing in all its forms. Until the industrial revolution, parish churches were closely related to the earth they stood on, a situation they gradually assumed from the pagan system which they had inherited. So for about two-and-a-half thousand years, the social unit had been the land-based parish.

Since the industrial revolution, the system of ecclesiastical tithing has been gradually dismantled because the nation's secular element has lost its faith in the national church's moral authority – the last legal threads were severed by parliament in 1996, a process which had been put in motion in 1936 – and it has not been soundly replaced. In the thriving days of tithing, everybody was directly involved in the process one way or another though some were very vexed by it, but now the valiant Parochial Church Councils bear the whole brunt. They enjoy much of it – the fêtes and the parties – but hate the hunt for legacies and sugar daddies because it is so degrading and it distracts everyone from the central spirit of the thing; it feels to them such a contradiction of their faith.

I heard from a member of the Wickham Market congregation two and a half miles down the valley that their annual budget of £100,000 was raised entirely from their members each paying a tenth of their annual incomes – a revitalised tithing system based not upon land but upon the zeal of the believers. The Rector expressed enthusiasm for the arrangement because, he said, they could dispense with money-raising events and get on with enjoying life! 'Besides,' said one of his flock with confidence, 'it's biblical!'

Wickham Market's heroism is noteworthy but their situation is different from places like Letheringham in almost every way. It certainly made me think. If, for example, Jo and I gave up our daily paper which is delivered, reduced our use of the phone, the electricity and the car by ten per cent, our food bills by fifteen per cent and wine bills by thirty per cent, we would each have about £1000 a year in hand. Not difficult. These simple economies would test our true commitment to the cause. And, if all the other Electoral Rollers resident in our particular parish did the same, for example, every penny of our church's expenditure would be found – maintaining the fabric as well as the running costs – and there would be a little left over for a party.

I looked up from my notes and prodded the neglected fire. I tidied the notes, tore them up and fed them to the flames. My chest was aching as I straightened, foolish to have spent so long with the thing. On Monday I would simply mention the little-known fact that the church itself belongs to the parish and it is the legal right of the parishioners, regardless of their private beliefs, to elect each spring two churchwardens fit enough to keep their church in good working order. They are obliged to elect them at the annual Easter Vestry. As electors they do not have to be on the Church Electoral Roll, or to be baptised. They merely have to be resident within the parish boundaries. The aspiring churchwardens however do have to be baptised and to be regular communicants at the church.

Churchwardens have always been influential people in the land. Their office is primarily a civil appointment, and a religious one secondarily. Their chief duties are, broadly speaking, to keep the building intact and to see that appropriate services are maintained. No hobgoblins or dragons, or even diocesan advisory councils, may redundantise their church against their wishes. Even the Chancellor of the Diocese is unlikely to act against the lawful representations of churchwardens genuinely expressing the wishes of the parishioners.

Because of these things, it is advisable that the Church Treasurer should keep two entirely separate accounts, one for the Fabric of the Building and the other for the Running Costs, for there are always some parishioners who would gladly write a cheque for the upkeep of the building but who may have little use for the local brand of church activities, sad though this may be.

There was a time when churchwardens raised funds by brewing beer, but later they were instructed to ensure that neither they nor anybody else should brew 'spirituous beverages', particularly 'in the tower'. There is however a rumour in Letheringham that Richard Overton who is one of the ginger group thinks the redundant Priory Gatehouse would make an excellent brewery. Who can tell what they'll get up to next?

Chapter 12
MARY

In my youth there was an argument in our village in Kent between two of the top gardeners about the best day to plant your potatoes: would Good Friday give them the liveliest resurrection or would Lady Day ensure a safer rebirth? Bemused, I preferred the latter but my mother who did most of the gardening said it was too Roman Catholic, not really English, and she was not joking.

Lady Day is the easy name for the Feast of the Annunciation of the Blessed Virgin Mary on 25th March (this very Sunday) celebrating since at least the seventh century the occasion when the Archangel Gabriel dropped in on Mary, a maiden, or maybe a servant girl, of Nazareth, and mentioned that she would be giving birth to an unusual child, a king no less, whose reign would last for ever. You can imagine her surprise. But according to St Luke who reported the event she took it well and, he implied, she seemed to be more concerned about being pregnant than about the king, for her only response was, 'How shall this be, seeing I know not a man?' She then packed her bags and went up into the hills to stay with her cousin Elizabeth. She was greeted with such rapture that she broke into song, a song of truly Jewish style and beauty praising the Almighty for his beneficence, a song which Christian priests have sung daily in their devotions ever since.

Mary gave birth and the rest is history. As a mother she suffered all the pangs and joys of parenthood – recorded in the four Gospels – and she was there at the gory end. But it was only at the birth that she took centre stage and it is for that she is chiefly remembered. She has survived, silent and serene, all the religious contortions of the centuries and now presides unobtrusively each mid-winter over that most extravagant of secular festivals. Even the noisiest of non-believers will dwell a pause when confronted with her image, he knows not why. Is it her unaffected modesty, her youth and vulnerability? Or is it the soothing blueness of her clothing and the magical triangle of her shape? Or is it simply her motherhood and the form of that infant she holds in the silent night? It is a mystery.

The Priory Church at Letheringham was named after this Mary, the saint above all others who they hoped would give it and them protection. She was to be their guardian in this world, their intercessor in the other. But today there is no representation of her image anywhere in our church. It is because a Mr Dowsing of Laxfield was employed in 1644 to destroy with his band of toughs all the 'popery' they could find in the churches of Suffolk, including 'ten superstitious pictures' at Letheringham, according to his diary. Of course, the puritanical element that employed such vandals as Dowsing felt justified by their faith but their crime was also political and commercial.

It is true to say that early Christians, following the Jews, were always uneasy about imagery, and indeed anything that is a substitute for the real thing. They encouraged their flocks to approach the Almighty 'face to face' undistracted by any form of 'vanity', and the Moslems in their turn followed suit with the utmost rigour. Yet later Christians have painted and carved on regardless.

The earliest depiction of the 'Virgin and Child' that I have heard of is in the Catacomb of Priscilla beneath Rome, a primitive daub of exquisite composure, a scene which has been repeated in all the world ever since; the Reformation in the West and the Iconoclasm in the East causing only slight local hesitations. In Letheringham the Georgian restorers, working on a tight budget, did not attempt to recover what had been destroyed, so we are left with an interior of immaculate whiteness that would offend neither Jew nor Moslem – nor any visitor in search of uncluttered peace and sobriety.

There are 151 other churches in the Suffolk diocese today which have been given Mary as their patron saint – a third of all the parish churches. In the eighth century there were only about twenty in the whole country but by the sixteenth century the number had increased to 'well over two thousand.' After Mary, the next most popular names in this diocese are All Saints (safety in numbers) with 72 churches, Peter (fisherman and allegedly first Bishop of Rome) with 53 churches, and Andrew (his quiet brother, also a fisherman) with 39 churches.

The third third of the parish churches is watched over by 46 further names of very wide variety. Most of the unfamiliar ones are to the west: Agnes, Denys, Giles, Genevieve, Petronilla, Patrick, for example, each with only one church. Other singles are Augustine of Hippo (the scholarly Tunisian bishop), Augustine of Canterbury (an Italian), Thomas à Becket (of Norman extraction), Charles (King and Martyr) and Francis – I wish he had more – (of Assisi).

The four Saxon heroes of East Anglia have a few churches between them: St Botolph, Abbot of Iken, has four: St Ethelbert, who was treacherously slain by the King of Mercia and his wife, has four; and St Edmund, slaughtered by Viking yobs in Hoxne and deemed by some today to be worthier of the patron-sainthood of England than St George. Yet George has six churches and under-rated Edmund only five. But poor 'tawdry St Audrey' (an unfair posthumous nickname for Ethelreda) has no Suffolk churches at all. She did have a famous mental hospital at Melton, near Woodbridge, till recently when it was converted into a posh housing estate and golf course. Ethelreda, a lonesome woman, founded Ely and is the patron saint of a dozen ancient churches elsewhere in the country.

St Felix – such a delightful name for a bishop – shares the church at Rumburgh with St Michael and has a whole town to himself between the mouths of the two rivers Deben and Orwell where a cluster of patron saints includes St Nicholas, a fourth-century bishop of dodgy origins who has twelve churches in the diocese. He was a thaumaturgist honoured in Eastern Orthodoxy as well as the West, and was made patron saint of both Greece and Russia, and of sailors, merchants, apothecaries, pawnbrokers (sporting his three balls) and children, now known to Americans as the rumbustious Santa Claus and as such, I suppose we have to concede, he has become a rather more familiar patron of Christmas than Our Lady of Letheringham.

Official lists of saints are of bewildering length and obscurity, and there are many more known only in the localities where they lived or died. Official calendars name nearly a thousand feast days and there were many more abandoned over the centuries yet their numbers still grow. The Book of Common Prayer has only ninety, thank goodness, and some of those look a bit dusty to me but only a score were considered significant enough to be given special prayers and readings for their feast days. Since the Reformation the English Church has regarded official sainthood with some reserve.

Christian saints started innocently enough in the catacombs with the fond messages, symbols and images scratched and painted on their tombs by their loved ones. Those heroes of the Roman persecutions who were widely recognised had haloes from the start. Once their body parts began to be traded by the commercial boys, the rot set in and perversions reached their ludicrous and scandalous crescendo in the Middle Ages.

In the catacombs there are many pictures of people feasting because they associated heaven with a great banquet where the Almighty himself presided and only the decent chaps were invited – the dirty cads would be chucked out, as everyone had always hoped. And the custom of the living was to have a party on the anniversary of the death, all gathered round the tomb. Hence the 'feast days' of the saints today, when usually only the name remains, I fear. My wife's first school after the War was a convent in Essex. Her mother told me that she came home early one day and said glumly it was because, 'It is the Reverend Mother's feast day, but there was no sign of a feast, not even a bun.' I never asked why the Reverend Mother had a feast day in the first place. I thought you had to be dead for that.

A curious thing about the church at Letheringham is its orientation. Its axis points 14° south of east, not due east. I have asked several people about this but, though there were plenty of theories, none could say for certain what it means. I liked best the theory that it was connected with the movements of the planet Venus, not the moon or the sun, and nothing to do with a magnetic compass, for there were none in AD1200. A congenial diocesan architect in Woodbridge agreed about the compass and thought the orientation might be due to medieval churches being built upon the foundations of previous, often pagan, places of worship but, he was sure, 'Nobody knows.' Another suggestion was that 14° would point to Jerusalem but, after glancing at an atlas, I felt this could not be so because it would land up in Crimea a thousand miles to the north; the angle would have to be doubled to reach down to Jerusalem. The commonest assumption is that churches point east, roughly, because that is the general direction of the rising sun, and this is the easiest theory. But upon reflection it seems to me not good enough: the sun only rises due east twice a year, in March and in September. His winter solstice in December is way over to the right, and way over to the left in June for his summer solstice. In February and October he does rise at 14° south of east but I cannot see any significance in it.

I must find out more about the planet Venus. I understand she has an eight-year cycle and, in terms of regularity, was the most dependable heavenly body for the ancients. They calculated their calendars, their husbandry and much else from her movements. They revered her and associated her with fecundity and birth. She was for them definitely female and motherly. By the term 'ancients' here I mean, within the context of these islands, the peoples who lived here between about 3,500 and 2,000BC. They were astronomers who made henges which were observatories, of which about three hundred have so far been found and which are unique to the British Isles. In Ireland, Scotland and the West several henges are associated with the 'Grooved Ware People' who are thought to have drifted this way after surviving the Mediterranean catastrophe of 3150BC. The mathematics and technology involved in the construction and use of the henges here was also variously employed across 'the known world' and, famously, in Egypt. This science was referred to as their 'wisdom' by later generations and is thought to have been remembered from before the catastrophe; Plato among others referred to it.

Astrology followed in step with their astronomy, and

the anthropomorphic mythology of such peoples as the Greeks and Romans stemmed from such beginnings. When eventually the Romans of the fourth century AD decided to stop beating up the Christians and to assimilate them instead, they went as far as they could with transferring the rapturous qualities of their own beloved goddess Venus onto that modest maiden of Nazareth: 'Theotokos' the Greeks had called her, 'the God-bearer', but when the Romans translated this into their Latin it became 'Mother of God' and stirred up a swarm of theological dissent. However the notion survives in the Church of Rome and a dozen feast days have ensued, the last two of which were formalised quite recently: in 1854 the feast of her 'immaculate conception' and in 1950 her 'bodily assumption into heaven'.

And so, I cannot yet explain 14° south of east. Nor can I tell for certain how the church at Letheringham came to be called St Mary's. And I cannot convincingly link the planet Venus with the church in any way. But I can contemplate the reverence that those ancient scientists showed for the mathematically beautiful movements of the planet Venus, and I can feel a really deep gratitude for the pure, unaffected prose of St Luke describing the Annunciation. I can also drink whenever I like the tall serenity of the Church of Our Lady of Letheringham.

Today however I was not feeling well enough to celebrate the Annunciation with them at Letheringham. I wondered if they were having a party. They often do. They are very good at it.

Chapter 13
THE FUTURE

That last night I hardly slept. I was too restless to read, unable to sit still. The others had returned from Gabriel's birthday party and gone early to bed. After an hour or two I put on a coat and went out for a walk. I walked up the hill under a waxing and irritable moon: she was hassled by high scurrying clouds and mocked by owls floating down into the meadows for the hunt. As I passed the chickens roosting high in their stable they muttered to each other, shifting about on their perches. Up in the wood, naked trees rattled fretfully in the wind above my head longing for spring but bothered by the fitful moon and, like me, ill at ease. The wood seemed much bigger than usual tonight, colder and inhospitable. I looked and listened through its jostling congregation. Beyond John Mann's wild pond a fox barked, and barked again not scenting my presence. I moved further into the wood away from the wind and, leaning my aching back against a swaying ash, it seemed more cordial. 'Lighten our darkness, we beseech thee, O Lord; and by thy great mercy defend us from all perils and dangers of this night ...' The words flew across from centuries past. Like swallows they knew their way. But I, feeling spare and seeing how the trees were busy with the elements, turned and wandered back home.

It was well past midnight and now, I realised at last, the very day had come on which I was to deliver the mardle! By the fire I sipped cocoa and looked in vain for messages in the flames. Then I took down a book of saints past and present, perchance to benefit from some ghostly counsel and advice, but was dismayed to learn that, long ago upon this very night, a weird Feast of St William of Norwich had been instituted. His ghastly ordeal did not console me at all and, snapping the book shut, I returned it to its shelf. The report went like this.

On the Monday before Easter exactly eight hundred and sixty-three years ago, on this night being 26th March, a twelve-year-old apprentice to a tanner in Norwich had not returned home. They sent out search parties but it was only on the Saturday that his lacerated body was discovered in nearby woodland. His hands and feet were deeply wounded and the crown of his head was gashed. They carried his body to the cathedral chapterhouse where his uncle Godwin declared he had been sacrificed in a Passover ritual by local Jews: crucified, he claimed. A cult started and the body was enshrined in the Martyr's Chapel where visions and miracles were said to follow. Soon the offerings of pilgrims became lavish and, although the High Sheriff and, for different reasons, two Popes denied both the involvement of Jews in the murder and the holiness of the victim, the cult flourished for over a hundred years. It was not until the value of the offerings shrivelled to only four pence that it was abandoned.

The boy's name was William. Apart from this hideous

pack of circumstances nothing more is known of him. A verger in the cathedral today could not say where his grave might be. I am told screen paintings depict him in the churches of Eye, Loddon and Worstead. That is all. But did I hear his screams in the wind that night?

The relevance of this poor boy to Letheringham is slim. His death occurred fifty years before their church was built and thirty-five miles to the north of it and, although none of the parishioners may have made a pilgrimage to his shrine, it does illustrate the sort of things that went on in their heads which they thought might render them some form of salvation. Charles Freeman says they would pray to such a 'saint' as William for some favour or other and, if it materialised, they would bend a coin and put it aside to take to the shrine. Bent coins could not be used for any other purpose than this. The Church's revenue from it was huge.

My thoughts ground around this awful story for a long time. I may have dozed off a little on the sofa but, oddly, resisted sleep. It was not simply the scandal of the money involved, nor the superstition, nor even the boy's murder that disturbed me most, but the lurid reminder of Christianity's perennial anti-Semitism. For, in my understanding, everything about the words and works of that wandering North-country Jew named Jesus of Nazareth, before the commercial boys took over in the fourth century, is good; in fact all the best things in Christianity are utterly Jewish it seems, and they are beautiful, humbling and ennobling to the onlooker. So I am sickened by the stupid contortions of the religious salesmen down the ages who have tweaked and meddled with his image before handing it down to us, a relic encrusted with their rusty crimes and superstitions, which now crumbles apart in my shaking hands.

I remember this delirium well. I was sweating and wanting water but could not rise. My thoughts went on gloomily to consider the folly of getting caught up in that little Christian temple at Letheringham whose praises I was set to sing in a few hours' time: my mind was split. Should I tell them to tear it down, obliterate it forever from the face of the earth?

Even at this stage it did not occur to me that I was ill. The pain would pass away at dawn ... a little fresh air ... some pruning in the orchard ... a good breakfast and all would be well. Or so I thought. And even now I cannot understand the psychology of my denial. Such was its strength that only when I found I could not stand up and get to within shouting distance of the sleeping family did I reach for the telephone and make the call which appears in the first sentence of this book.

*

This book is a written account of the mardle which I failed to deliver in the evening of Monday 26th March 2007 and it has taken far too long to assemble. Some of the drugs they gave me after those miraculous operations made me lethargic and melancholic. The legend has expanded quite naturally beyond the bounds of a talk. Now it is May 2010, the task is nearly complete and I am well again thanks to those brilliant medical people.

Back in Letheringham a new priest has long since been appointed for the eight parishes, a lovely big smiling man who turns up at all the main events and never seems to get ruffled. His name is Dr. Stephen Brian, a Middlesex man, a teacher by trade who has been ordained for nearly twenty-five years now. The Ginger Group at Letheringham continues to organise life there. In April the Bishop of Dunwich mounted the tiny pulpit, resplendent in his scarlet and white, to dedicate Tessa's felicitous triptych and deliver a lively flow of thought and charm. He quoted Richard Overton's remark that this sort of art was in itself an act of worship. We all sang a translation of St Francis of Assisi's 'Canticle of Brother Sun'. It was a glorious day. Other than that, the services, the festivals, the mardles and the parties have continued in their unique and undaunted style.

I had told Polly that in my mardle I wanted to talk about the future, among other things, and she had said I may. I thought they would be entertained at the end if I made a fool of myself. For who can say what will happen in the next ten years? In the next ten minutes? But I do know, as certainly as anyone can know anything, that the natural world is growing exceedingly tired of humankind and is noticeably beginning to check us. Lots of people know this. You don't have to be a genius or a clairvoyant, but it helps if you work with plants and animals or make useful things out of natural materials. And when I compare the rude fecundity of the countryside in my youth with today's relatively barren landscape, I know the graphs are about to plummet, not all at once but gradually, like a giant lying down, limb by limb, painfully. Because we are little, we do not register the spectacle as a possible death and, because we are silly, we deny what we see and leave the remedy for others to supply.

It is also easier to foresee the 'Great Global Collapse' if you are old. Old people have always been good at moaning on about things. But this is different. We are the first to be looking at the exhaustion of Earth's resources, and the first to see a fast-expanding world population with a ravenous appetite for the extravagant luxuries which we in this country have taken for granted for a long time. It has happened before but on a much smaller scale.

Globalisation is the citification of the whole world, where an individual's wellbeing is dependent upon the health of the vast whole. When the vast whole collapses, as it must do, weakened by over-growing, we will have to creep back into the sobriety of villages and small towns where the individual health of such cellular communities will be within the limits of our collective grasp again. Recovery will be possible but the transition will probably be uncomfortable. For few of us will abandon our present, precious 'standard of living' voluntarily. Few will have prepared themselves either materially or mentally, and few will see the changes as a liberation or a blessing in disguise. Consequently many will die, dragged down by debility and dudgeon.

But the recovery in some places could be an orderly withdrawal in the best military tradition, given good leadership, rather than an ignominious retreat. And among the survivors will be people like the churchmongers of Letheringham, weaned on the nectar of the Nazareth man and toughened with his cool teaching about life on earth 'as it is in heaven'. Such people really are the practical ones, workers, down-to-earth and optimistic like the 'naughty' monks who built their church. They know their place. And if they keep their mardling going they will become like the original academicians of Greece, who sat under the trees in their orchards to thrash out their theories and their differences in debate: searchers and watchers of things beyond yet part of the flow of life, at home in the world, survivors. And their little church will survive with them. Surely they will see to that, they and those who follow.

*

So much for the future! Now we are approaching the middle of 2012 and publication. Two more summers have ticked by. In March last year I finally delivered the dreaded mardle, four years late and very altered. It was received by about seventy people enthusiastically, though some were a bit shaken in places. I had tried to cover too much ground and, being nervous, kept losing the thread and missing out important things. There was, alas, no time for questions but the audience was forgiving. So in the long run I hope this diary will have done what the talking could not do.

At various stages in the making, people have kindly read the script and said what they thought and so it was altered. Most of those to whom it refers have read it, or parts of it. So it is the product of a long process of metamorphosis, which was intended, because I wanted to present the building as a combination of their views. For such a place is much more than materials put there by its builders – although that alone is impressive – and it is much more than the deeds of the celebrities whose names may populate our history books. It incorporates another ingredient which each generation has known: its use by the unnamed, uncounted people who have entered it for one reason or another. Consider, if only one person a day had been into that holy place since it was built, we would be looking at over a quarter of a million pilgrims. This is difficult to imagine, but if we stood them up in the fields around the church and gave each of them about five square yards in which to have their being they would fill all the fields in the north corner of the parish (from the south side of Cutler's Grove and Office Farm down to the Forge Cottages and Fair Field and along to the Hoo Road behind the church), an area of nearly 300 acres. This area, incidentally, is roughly all you can see of the parish from the tower, just one quarter of its realm. The total number of visitors must of course be far larger than this and, if we could delve beyond the day it was built into its pre-history, the number of every sort of 'pilgrim' would be astronomical. As I see it, all of them have contributed something to what we find there today, although precisely what this is we cannot tell. John Brentnall said he felt that the church had 'a strong hush factor' – might this have been what he was talking about? Does a sort of radiation from their presence accumulate in its stones? Or was there already some sort of energy in the earth of the place which attracted its first settlers? Something akin to the phenomenon of migrating birds? Or to the culture of bees?

And after all that, having guessed at the number of human pilgrims, how on earth do we begin to estimate the number of attendant angels?

*

I have tried to represent the views of my fellow men and women who live around Letheringham today – and of the younger generations in particular, because they are the future – and I have tried to compare what they said with some of the teachings contained in that building. In the attempt, I have tumbled to the realisation that these two entities (the inclinations of the people and the teachings of the Church) were already surprisingly alike. Sometimes only their language seemed to separate them – as it does between scientists and theologians. The whole exercise has turned out to be a series of exhilarating lessons for me.

The last person to have read the script remarked, 'You've discovered what you believe, having questioned it all your life.' This is quite true, for previously my faith had been hung on hooks, put there by others. But now I am different. That little old church with her people has largely brought me to my own senses.

Page one asserted that I had blissfully surrendered my soul to the Almighty, while at the same time – as the Polite Outsider might have observed – I was feebly handing my body over to persons unknown. The outcome was beyond my reach. But those clever medical people – the consultant, the surgeon and the local doctors with their teams – are the ones to be thanked for my physical survival. They performed their magic on my body and I awoke to find that the peaceful grave had receded and my apparent life on this planet had been restored. Furthermore, as time passed, my relish for this life has increased and many of the anxieties that caused the illness have ebbed. So for all these things – the physical recovery as well as the diverse discoveries through that dear church and her people – I find no difficulty in giving most humble and hearty thanks to the Lord Above.

BIBLIOGRAPHY

Akenfield, Ronald Blythe (1969). Enchanting, essential.

Historical Atlas of Suffolk, David Dymond and Edward Martin (eds.) (SCC Planning Department, 1988). Brilliant.

Study of Land in the Upper Deben Valley, Gwen Dyke (c. 1977). Very interesting indeed.

The Celts (1971) and *The Druids* (1966), Nora Chadwick. Reliable history and basic information.

The Founder of Christianity, C. H. Dodd (1970). Scholarly yet within my reach.

A New History of Early Christianity, Charles Freeman (2009). Enthralling, as was his *AD381*.

The Year 1000, Robert Lacey and Danny Danziger (1999). Marvellous, delightful.

One Volume Bible Commentary, William Neil (1962). Indispensable for me.

Daily Telegraph Book of Hymns, Ian Bradley (2005). Fascinating, very useful.

Oxford Dictionary of the Christian Church, F. L. Cross (ed.) (1958). Essential.

A Detection of the Trinity, John Thurmer (1984) Stimulating academic theology.

Cycles of Time, Roger Penrose (2010). An extraordinary new view of the universe, stimulating science, fairly beyond my reach.